The Pumpkin & Squash Cookbook

The
Pumpkin & Squash
Cookbook

Rosemary Moon

APPLE

A QUINTET BOOK

Published by The Apple Press
6 Blundell Street
London N7 9BH

ISBN 1-84092-104-8

This book was designed and produced by
Quintet Publishing Limited
6 Blundell Street
London N7 9BH

Creative Director: Richard Dewing
Art Director: Silke Braun
Designer: Rita Wüthrich
Senior Editor: Sally Green
Editor: Rosie Hankin
Photographer: Ferguson Hill
Food Stylist: Kathryn Hawkins

Typeset in Great Britain by
Central Southern Typesetters, Eastbourne
Manufactured in Singapore by Pica Colour Separation Overseas Pte Ltd.
Printed in Singapore by Star Standard Industries Pte Ltd.

Contents

Introduction • 6

Soups, Starters and Relishes • 17

Salads • 35

Fish Dishes • 53

Meat and Poultry Dishes • 71

Main Course Vegetable Dishes • 93

Desserts and Baking • 109

Index/Acknowledgements • 127

Introduction

Cucumbers, melons pumpkins and squashes are all part of the same family as gourds, and it is highly likely that hard-skinned, prickly gourds were used as weapons long before anyone thought of eating them or their relatives. What is certain is that they were growing between three and five thousand years ago in Peru, but it is assumed that they were originally native to Africa. The most popular theory for their arrival in South America is that they were carried by Polynesian voyagers crossing the great oceans. Many centuries later, they were 'discovered' by Columbus and the Spanish, and taken to Europe.

Gourds have featured in the ancient history of peoples around the world. In India they were used as water carriers, and they are mentioned in Chinese history some 400 years before Confucius. It is therefore thought by some that, because the seeds of the whole family are so durable, they may well have been washed from one continent to another by the sea. Whatever the truth of the matter, it is indisputable that gourds, pumpkins and squashes are popular and valuable crops throughout the world.

Although pumpkins, squashes, cucumbers and melons are all related, they are a diverse range of fruits. The distinction between them is more based on area of origin: pumpkins and squashes are native to the New World of the Americas, and the word 'squash' is from the American Indian word *askutasquash*; melons and cucumbers, however, were known of in or before Old Testament times in the Old World, and are generally grouped into the family of gourds, a word coming from the Latin *cucurbita*. So, you might argue that an American harvest would comprise only pumpkins and squashes, based on origins, but as cucumbers, marrows and melons are enjoyed throughout the world, I have kept the family together within the pages of this book, although pumpkins and squashes are definitely the main ingredients.

Gourds are usually much smaller than pumpkins and squashes and may be edible or decorative. They are often fascinating in shape—

Above *Everyone is familiar with the large orange pumpkins, used as lanterns at Halloween.*

Right *A fine display of pumpkins and squashes, including many varieties from around the world.*

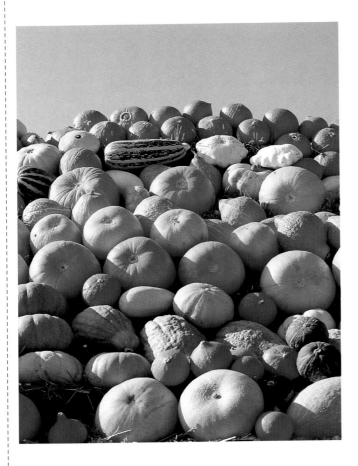

Pumpkins and squashes are both edible and decorative.

crook necked, penguin, or bottle shaped, smooth-skinned, warty, and possibly multicoloured. Throughout history they have been put to decorative or practical uses—water carriers, storage pots, vases, musical instruments, rattles and lamp bases. The chayote is one of the best known edible gourds, and was originally grown in South and Central America, but is now popular in China as well, where it is sliced and stir-fried. I have not included edible gourds in this book as there was so much to say about the commoner edible fruits.

For many years the perception of pumpkins has been of a rather bland ingredient, watery and without much flavour—something to make into a pie at Thanksgiving or a lantern for Halloween. But the members of this fruit family are extremely versatile—they are good in savoury dishes, and also excellent in pies and ice creams too. As I have explored the varieties of pumpkins and squashes for my recipes, and experimented on friends and family, we have all reached the same conclusion: they are deliciously versatile and we should all be far more adventurous with them. I hope my recipes will inspire you in your kitchen.

Pumpkin Varieties

I really don't think that as cooks we need to get side-tracked into the business of classifying the foods we eat into their correct scientific or botanical families. However, some basic knowledge of the varieties can be quite useful. For example, the big orange pumpkin that we all think of for lanterns and soup is *Cucurbita pepo*, as are the spaghetti marrow or squash, courgettes and other soft-skinned varieties. These are summer squashes and do not store well. Winter varieties, such as acorn, butternut, crown prince and Hubbard all have harder skins and do store—through the winter—and are *Cucurbita maxima* or *Cucurbita moschata*. Most winter squashes can be substituted one for another in recipes, although you will quickly find which is your favourite and go back to that time and again.

Growing Pumpkins

All melons, cucumbers, pumpkins and marrows grow on sprawling, vine-like plants, although modern bush varieties take up slightly less room, or may be trained upward to economize on space in the garden. Pumpkins and marrows, including courgettes, are generally easy to cultivate but they do take up a vast amount of room, especially if it is your dream to grow the award-winning, biggest pumpkin of all time. They like lots of sun and nutrient-rich soil, which is why they are often found trailing over the compost heap. They also need a lot of water. To ensure the maximum time for the fruits to develop, it is best to sow the seeds under glass and bring the plants on at the beginning of the season, before hardening them off after the last frost and then planting them out. No members of this family like frost at the beginning or end of their lives.

If you buy a squash or pumpkin that you particularly like, it is always worth saving a few seeds from it to grow on the next year. In order to get large fruits I always restrict my pumpkins to about four fruits a plant, pinching out or stopping the shoots after the fruits have set, so that all the goodness and effort is concentrated on the tasks of growing and ripening. If you intend to store squashes for later use, they should be left in the sun for 10 to 14 days after cutting, to allow the skins to harden. This will encourage them to keep well in a frost-free, ventilated shed.

Cucumbers and melons are also grown on vines, but they tend to be trained in an upright habit in greenhouses to achieve the necessary temperatures. Melons need to be supported as they ripen—the fruits can get very heavy—and keen gardeners will have net hammocks or slings for them. (A pair of tights may serve as a substitute.)

Armenian cucumber growing on the vine.

Cucumbers are either smooth-skinned and long (these varieties must be grown under glass) or smaller and ridged. The latter, which I find to be slightly more bitter in flavour, may be grown outside. Cucumbers may be straight or curved. There are some unusual varieties, including tiny, prickly round ones, sometimes called hairy spiky cucumbers, although also known as squirting cucumbers, because of their method of ejecting their seeds for distribution. The massive Armenian cucumbers which have a speckled green and cream flesh are known, accurately, as Armenian yard-longs, whereas regular Armenian varieties only grow to 40–45 cm/16–18 inches. Lebanese cucumbers are a similar shape, dark green in colour but grow only about 20–23 cm/8–9 inches long. And the baby of them all, the Jamaican, is apple green in colour, egg shaped and only about 4 cm/1½ inches long.

A melon ripening in the net.

Ripeness in Melons

The most useful tip that I can offer with regard to selecting a ripe and juicy melon is that they will be fragrant when ready to eat. Only press a melon gently at the end—it should give a little—otherwise the flesh will bruise, but do sniff before buying at the supermarket. This works well for most varieties except honeydews, which have a harder, more impermeable skin. Ripe melons should be seductively fragrant.

Probably the only way to be certain of the sweetness and juiciness of a watermelon before cutting into it is by looking at the stalk. When the flesh is ready to eat it should be slightly sunken into the top of the melon, and roughened with bumps. Of course, if it has been trimmed ready for sale this is no guide at all.

Pumpkins and squashes are native to the warmer parts of the Americas, but they are now grown successfully in many parts of the world, and are a popular, as well as economically important, crop.

United States

Without doubt the most common variety in the United States is the big, orange pumpkin. That's a bit of a loose description, as there are actually lots of different varieties that are all very similar. Because they are watery in comparison to the firmer squashes, I prefer not to boil them as they can very easily cook to a mush. Dice and steam them if you will, or cook in olive oil or butter with freshly grated nutmeg or black pepper. They are also good in soups, especially when combined with a stronger-flavoured vegetable, such as carrot or swede. The cooked flesh may also be puréed and used in numerous sweet or savoury dishes.

Orange pumpkins

Of all the squashes the butternut is one of the most popular. It is native to tropical America, but is now widely cultivated in the north. It is naturally pear-shaped, although it may remain cylindrical if growing conditions are not quite warm enough. The flesh is dramatically orange, and it bakes, roasts and stews well. It is one of my favourite varieties for soups, especially with orange. The banana squash is very good for curries as it is dry and firm-fleshed, and retains its shape when cooked. Another American variety, the golden nugget, is usually eaten when young with a soft skin. The flesh has a green tinge and it may be stuffed and baked like a marrow.

The acorn squash can be green or yellow or both.

Canada

The most famous of the Canadian squashes is the acorn, although this is now also very popular next door in the United States. Acorns are usually green-skinned, but they do turn yellow. They are hard-skinned and ridged, which makes them very difficult to peel before cooking. I usually cut them in half to bake, or cut them into rings to fry. The skin can be cut off easily once the flesh is cooked. Blue Hubbards, which have very hard, warty skins, grow to be very large indeed and can be very difficult to cut into although, strangely enough, rabbits seem to have no difficulty in munching their way into them. This Canadian variety is also widely grown elsewhere.

Australia and New Zealand

The most famous of the Australian varieties is the Queensland blue which, like the blue Hubbard, can grow to an enormous size. It has a very good flavour and texture, and becomes really creamy when mashed with butter after boiling or steaming. The snake squash is native to Australia and Southeast Asia, and is pale green in colour. Because it grows like a curled snake it is best eaten young, when the skin is tender, so that it can be sliced into distinctive rounds before cooking. The flavour is greatly enhanced by herbs.

Some of my favourite squashes are native to New Zealand, where they are promoted as an excellent vegetable for the modern health-conscious diet. My number one favourite is the crown prince, a

Right *Crown prince squashes are native to New Zealand.*

Kabocha squashes

Onion squash

Gem squash

smooth, hard-skinned variety with a grey skin and vibrant orange flesh. It pan-fries and stir-fries well, it bakes and roasts, and it makes full-flavoured, smooth soups. Crown prince is also very tasty cold, making it an excellent choice for salads.

Other New Zealand varieties include the buttercup (also popular in the United States) and the kabocha. The latter is usually green-skinned and, like the crown prince, has bright orange flesh. It bakes and fries well, and I often use it in breads. The red kabocha is less well known but some consider it to have a finer and more distinctive flavour than the standard variety.

Japan

Popular in New Zealand, but also a firm favourite in Japan, the uchiki kuri is more popularly known as the onion squash, especially in the West. It is easy to see how this name evolved, as the deep orange skin has very distinct onion markings. The squash is best baked after scooping out the seeds. I sometimes start it off in a hot oven, then add a filling. Cover with foil, at least for part of the cooking time, to prevent the flesh from drying out before it is tender. Another popular Japanese squash is the kumikuri, an orange and green variety with orange ribs.

South Africa

Squashes are very popular in South Africa, and some of the best known are the butternut, the golden Hubbard, and the tiny round gem squash. Gems are best pierced two or three times with a fork and then boiled—scoop the seeds out once the squash is cooked. They can also be peeled and sliced, and then fried.

The rolet, which is very similar to the gem, is actually native to Zimbabwe and is cooked in the same way. The skin is a slightly deeper green but, apart from that, I can detect very little difference between the two.

France

Pumpkins are very popular in France. The French prefer ridged, deep orange pumpkins to the paler varieties, and they also grow many Turk's caps, an orange squash with a striped green and white centre which gives this distinctive variety its name. Although it is delicious to eat and may be stuffed, once well coloured and ripened, the skin will harden and become very difficult to cut. Many people end up using these colourful squashes simply for decorative purposes.

Cooking the Squash Recipes

Many of my recipes start by roasting pumpkin or squash before going on to use it in other ways. I have a big range cooker at home which is always on, so I simply roast slices of squash in the constantly hot oven before I purée or chop the flesh. However, to put an ordinary oven on just for this would be rather extravagant. If you are using the oven and there is a little room to spare, even if the oven is set at a lower temperature, do take the opportunity to roast or bake some pumpkin or squash slices for later use. Just cook them until they are tender. They keep well when wrapped up in the refrigerator—indeed they keep better that way than leaving a cut pumpkin out in the kitchen.

Sliced or diced pumpkin and squash may also be steamed if you prefer, or cooked in the microwave. Microwave cookbooks will suggest a suitable timing, but it would generally be about 5 minutes on High per 0.5 kg/1 lb depending on the oven. Microwave cooking is more suitable for preparing the flesh for purées than for salads—diced squash or pumpkin could be pan-fried for the latter use, although this may increase the fat content of the finished dish.

Cutting Pumpkins and Squashes

One reason why I roast the pumpkin or squash for so many of my recipes is that it makes actually peeling the skin away so much easier. Some of the winter squash varieties, especially those with very hard skins, can be very difficult to cut into and to peel. I find that the best knife to use is a butcher's knife, with a slightly rounded end to the blade. This seems to give slightly better leverage than the more traditional cook's knife. A cleaver would undoubtedly make the task of the initial cut somewhat easier—but do take care! Persevere—the following recipes prove that the effort expended in preparation really is worthwhile.

Pumpkin Seeds— a Delicious Nibble

I have never actually toasted squash seeds—they seem rather hard—but pumpkin seeds do make an excellent nibble, a good alternative to peanuts.

Scrape them out of the pumpkin and pull off any stringy flesh, then wash them well and leave them to dry on absorbent kitchen paper.

Once dry, the seeds can be grilled, or dry-fried in a nonstick frying pan.

Season them while still hot— I usually just add milled sea salt—then toss them from time to time in the seasoning until completely cold.

Munch immediately, or store in a screw-top jar.

Chilled Cucumber and Green Chile Soup

Roasted Acorn Soup with Cucumber Salsa

Mediterranean Roasted Pumpkin Soup

Butternut and Orange Soup

Pumpkin, Lentil, and Bacon Soup

Melon and Pesto Soup

Pumpkin, Carrot, and Lovage Soup

Baked Gem Squash with Parmesan Cream

Baked Limed Zucchini in Cream

Melon with Figs and Prosciutto

Pumpkin, Bacon, and Tomato Skewers

Roast Crown Prince Squash and Pistachio Pâté

Curried Lamb and Pumpkin Koftas

Spiced Minted Melon Balls

Pumpkin Chutney

Butternut and Chicken Liver Pâté

Pumpkin Relish

Cucumber and Radish Raita

Chilled Cucumber and Green Chilli Soup

This soup is highly spiced which counteracts the 'flavour numbing' effect of chilling. Traditional Thai seasonings make it very refreshing.

SERVES 6

- 4 large spring onions, trimmed and sliced
- 1 stalk lemon grass, bruised and finely chopped
- 1–2 garlic cloves, crushed
- 2 each green and caribe chillies, seeded and finely chopped, or 3 green chillies
- 2 lime leaves, finely shredded
- 1 vegetable stock cube, crumbled
- 900 ml/1½ pints water
- 1 large cucumber, weighing about 450 g/1 lb, seeded and chopped
- 250 ml/9 fl oz natural yogurt
- 1 Tbsp fish sauce
- Salt, to taste
- 2 Tbsp chopped fresh coriander leaves

Preparation: 1 hour 10 minutes
Chilling time: 2–3 hours

❶ Place the spring onions, lemon grass, garlic, chillies and lime leaves in a large saucepan with the crumbled stock cube. Pour in the water, then bring to the boil. Add the cucumber, then cover the pan completely and remove from the heat, and leave to marinate for 1 hour.

❷ Purée the soup in a blender or food processor until smooth, then press the mixture through a fine sieve with the back of a ladle. Whisk in the yogurt and fish sauce, then season the soup to taste with a little salt if necessary. Chill very well, for at least 2 hours.

❸ Add the coriander to the soup just before serving, and spoon the soup over about a tablespoon of crushed ice in each individual bowl.

TIP

Fresh herbs have been used throughout this book. However, dried herbs could always be substituted. Use 1 tsp dried for every Tbsp fresh herbs.

soups, starters & relishes

Roasted Acorn Soup with Cucumber Salsa

This creamy, nutty flavoured soup is further enhanced by a subtly spicy cucumber salsa.

SERVES 4

- 1 acorn squash (weighing about 575 g/1¼ lb) quartered
- Salt and freshly grated nutmeg
- Olive oil
- 1 large onion, finely chopped
- 2 rashers back bacon, rinded and chopped
- 2 large carrots, sliced
- 4–5 young lovage leaves, finely shredded, or 3 bay leaves
- 900 ml/1½ pints well-flavoured vegetable stock
- Ground black pepper
- 250 ml/9 fl oz milk

FOR THE SALSA

- 1 Tbsp coriander seeds
- ½ medium cucumber, seeded and diced
- 1 mild green chilli, seeded and very finely chopped
- 1 small red onion, finely chopped
- 1 fresh tomato, seeded and chopped
- 1 garlic clove, finely chopped
- 2.5 cm/1-inch piece fresh root ginger, coarsely grated

Preparation: 50 minutes
Cooking time: 45 minutes

---

❶ Preheat a 220°C/425°F/gas mark 7 oven. Scrape the seeds out of the squash, then arrange the pieces in a roasting tin, and season lightly with salt and nutmeg. Drizzle with a little olive oil, then roast the squash for 45 minutes, or until tender. Then leave to cool.

❷ Meanwhile, cook the onion, bacon and carrots with 1 tablespoon of olive oil in a covered pan for 4 to 5 minutes, until the vegetables are tender. Scoop the roasted squash from the skin, chop it roughly, then add it to the pan with the lovage or bay, and stock. Season lightly with salt and pepper, then bring to the boil. Cover the pan and simmer for 30 minutes.

❸ Meanwhile, prepare the salsa. Heat a small frying pan over medium heat until hot, then add the coriander seeds and fry for about 1 minute, until roasted and fragrant. Crush the seeds lightly using a pestle and mortar, or use the end of a rolling pin. Add all the other salsa ingredients except the ginger. Finally, gather up the ginger shreds in your hands and squeeze just the juice into the mixture. Leave to stand for about 30 minutes, to allow the flavours to blend.

❹ Cool the soup slightly, then blend until smooth in a blender or food processor, adding the milk. Season to taste and reheat if necessary. Serve the soup with a generous spoonful of salsa in each portion.

TIP
Roasting hard-skinned squashes before their final cooking has two advantages: it makes them easier to cut and prepare and it brings out their naturally nutty flavour.

soups, starters & relishes

Mediterranean Roast Pumpkin Soup

A really lively soup to serve before an equally powerful main course! Blend the olives into the soup if you prefer.

SERVES 4

- 6 x 2.5-cm/1-in slices pumpkin, seeded (about 750 g/1 lb 10 oz in total)
- 6 large tomatoes, halved
- 1 large onion, thickly sliced
- 4–5 garlic cloves
- 4 sprigs fresh rosemary
- Salt and ground black pepper
- Olive oil
- 450 ml/¾ pints water or stock
- 75 g/3 oz stoned black olives, chopped
- Shavings of fresh Parmesan cheese
- Olive oil bread, to serve

Preparation: 10 minutes
Cooking time: 1 hour

❶ Preheat a 220°C/425°F/gas mark 7 oven. Arrange the vegetables in a large roasting tin and tuck in the rosemary. Season well, then drizzle with olive oil. Roast for 40 to 50 minutes, until starting to blacken. Allow the vegetables to cool.

❷ Cut the flesh away from the skin of the pumpkin and chop roughly.

Remove the rosemary, then scrape all the vegetables into a blender or food processor, and add the pumpkin flesh. Blend until smooth, then rub the soup through a fine sieve into a saucepan.

❸ Add the water or stock, then heat the soup slowly until almost at the boil. Season, then stir in the chopped olives. Ladle into warmed bowls, and garnish with a few shavings of Parmesan.

Butternut and Orange Soup

This was one of the first squash dishes that I ever tasted and has remained a firm favourite ever since!

SERVES 4–6

- 1 onion, chopped
- 2 Tbsp olive oil
- 1–2 butternut squashes (about 900 g/2 lb in total), peeled, diced
- Grated rind and juice of 2 oranges
- 1.5 litres/2½ pints well-flavoured vegetable stock
- Salt and ground black pepper
- 2 bay leaves
- Freshly grated nutmeg
- 2 Tbsp chopped fresh parsley

Preparation: 10 minutes
Cooking time: 45 minutes

❶ Cook the onion in the oil until softened, then add the squash and cook slowly for 5 minutes, stirring occasionally. Stir in the grated orange, then add the stock, seasoning, bay leaves and nutmeg. Bring the soup to the boil, then cover and simmer for 40 minutes, until the squash is tender.

❷ Allow the soup to cool slightly, remove the bay leaves, then blend in a blender or food processor until smooth. Rinse the pan and return the soup to it, adding the orange juice. Reheat the soup slowly—do not let it boil—then season to taste, and add the freshly chopped parsley just before serving.

Mediterranean Roast Pumpkin Soup

Pumpkin, Lentil and Bacon Soup

Lentils and bacon add a smokey flavour to this creamy pumpkin soup.

SERVES 4–6

- 1 onion, finely chopped
- 4 rashers smoked back bacon, rinded and chopped
- 2 Tbsp olive oil
- 2 garlic cloves, sliced fine
- 400 g/14 oz pumpkin, peeled, seeded and diced
- 100 g/4 oz red lentils
- 400-g/14-oz can chopped tomatoes
- 4 sprigs fresh thyme
- 2 bay leaves
- Salt and ground black pepper
- 900 ml/1½ pints well-flavoured vegetable stock
- 150 ml/¼ pint whipping cream

Preparation: 15 minutes
Cooking time: 40 minutes

---

❶ Cook the onion and bacon in the oil for 5 minutes over low heat, until the onions are soft but not browned. Add the garlic and the pumpkin, and cook for 2 minutes more, then stir in the lentils.

❷ Add the seasonings, then pour in the stock. Bring the soup to the boil, then simmer slowly for 30 to 40 minutes, until the pumpkin and lentils are tender.

❸ Allow the soup to cool slightly, then remove the thyme and bay leaves, before blending in a blender or food processor until smooth. Add extra salt and pepper to taste, then ladle the soup into warmed bowls. Add a swirl of cream to each helping before serving.

Melon and Pesto Soup

A chilled melon soup that is perfect for summer entertaining as it actually benefits from being made up to a day in advance. The pesto redeems the flavour of the fruit beautifully. It's also a marvellous way of using up the shells of melons that you have balled for other dishes.

SERVES 4

- 900 ml/1½ pints Galia melon purée (made from 2 melons)
- 1 mild green chilli, seeded and very finely chopped
- 150 ml/¼ pint water
- 3 Tbsp best quality pesto sauce
- Salt and white pepper
- Lime juice, to taste

Preparation: 15 minutes
Chilling time: 2 hours

---

❶ Blend the melon purée with all the remaining ingredients, adding just enough lime juice to lift the flavour of the soup.

❷ Chill the soup for at least 2 hours, then serve over a little crushed ice. Crisp toasts made with Italian bread and flavoured with a mild garlic butter are a perfect accompaniment.

TIP

It is essential to use the very best pesto sauce—it should be slightly sweet, and made just with basil, garlic, Parmesan, pine nuts and olive oil.

Melon and Pesto Soup

Pumpkin, Carrot and Lovage Soup

I like to add carrots to this soup, to give a little more texture and flavour as I use the main crop orange pumpkin. This is an excellent recipe for using up the inside of a Halloween pumpkin.

SERVES 6

- 1 large onion, chopped
- 3 Tbsp olive oil
- 400 g/14 oz pumpkin, peeled, seeded and diced
- 250 g/9 oz carrots, diced
- 1 Tbsp chopped fresh lovage or 2 Tbsp chopped fresh flat-leafed parsley
- 2 bay leaves
- 1 litre/1¾ pints well-flavoured vegetable stock
- Salt and ground black pepper
- Single cream, to serve

Preparation: 15 minutes
Cooking time: 30 minutes

❶ Cook the onion in the oil until softened but not browned, then add the pumpkin and carrots, and continue cooking for about 5 minutes. Stir in the lovage or parsley, bay leaves and stock, then bring the soup gradually to the boil. Season well, then cover the pan and simmer for 30 minutes, until all the vegetables are tender.

❷ Allow the soup to cool slightly, then remove the bay leaves. Blend until smooth in a blender or food processor. Return the soup to the pan and stir in a little extra stock to thin the soup, if necessary. Season again, reheat gently, then serve with a generous swirl of cream.

Baked Gem Squash with Parmesan Cream

Gem squash are tiny, the jewels of the pumpkin world. Baked with a rich mixture of cream, Parmesan and garlic, they make the most wonderful but simple starter.

SERVES 4

- 4 gem squash, halved and seeded
- Olive oil
- 300 ml/½ pint single cream
- 100 g/4 oz freshly grated Parmesan cheese
- 1 mild green chilli, seeded and chopped fine
- 1–2 garlic cloves, crushed
- Pinch of ground mace (optional)
- Salt and ground black pepper

Preparation: 10 minutes
Cooking time: 30 minutes

❶ Preheat a 200°C/400°F/gas mark 6 oven. Score the flesh of the squash deeply, then drizzle with olive oil. Mix the cream with the cheese, and all the remaining ingredients, then pour the mixture into the squashes.

❷ Bake for 30 minutes, until the squash is tender. Serve immediately with a salad leaf and tomato garnish.

Baked Gem Squash with Parmesan Cream

Baked Limed Courgettes in Cream

Limes and courgettes are very amenable partners. This is almost a savoury baked custard—a crème caramel without the sugar topping.

SERVES 4

- 150 ml/¼ pint single cream
- 2 kaffir lime leaves, shredded
- 250 g/9 oz courgettes, grated
- Grated rind and juice of 1 lime
- 1 garlic clove, crushed
- Freshly grated nutmeg
- 1 large egg, beaten
- Salt and ground black pepper
- 2 Tbsp toasted breadcrumbs

Preparation: 35 minutes
Cooking time: 35 minutes

---

❶ Heat the cream with the lime leaves in a small saucepan or in a jug in the microwave until hot but not boiling. Leave for 20 minutes to infuse, then remove the lime leaves.

❷ Preheat a 170°C/325°F/gas mark 3 oven. Mix all the ingredients together with the flavoured cream,

then divide the mixture between four buttered ramekin dishes. Place the ramekins in a small roasting tin, then half fill the pan with boiling water. Bake the creams for 30 to 35 minutes.

❸ Remove the creams from the roasting tin and leave to cool for 5 minutes. Scatter toasted crumbs over each ramekin, then serve warm.

Melon with Figs and Parma Ham

Do I like ripe, juicy figs best with melon, or is my favourite accompaniment wafer-thin slices of moist Parma ham? I can never decide—so I have both! This 'arrangement' is easy to achieve.

SERVES 4

- 12 thin slices of ripe fragrant melon, such as Charentais or cantaloupe
- 8–12 wafer-thin slices Parma ham
- 4 ripe figs
- Spanish olive oil (optional)
- Ground black pepper
- Fresh coriander, to garnish

Preparation: 15 minutes

---

❶ Fan out the melon on individual plates, arranging the ham over the slices or interleaving them.

❷ Cut the figs into four—but not quite through to the base—then push slightly upward from the base to open. Add the figs to the plates.

❸ Drizzle a little olive oil over the arrangement. Season the ham and fig with pepper, then garnish with coriander before serving.

TIP

Do not chill this starter as the luxurious flavours will be stifled by the cold. Also, only set out the ham out when you are ready to serve, as it dries out very quickly. The melon and the fig, however, may be prepared in advance, and the dish is finished in just about a minute or two.

soups, starters & relishes

Pumpkin, Bacon and Tomato Skewers

A light but very tasty starter of orange pumpkin and bacon—always a winning combination—with tomatoes and Parmesan cheese. Serve on a bed of rice to make a slightly more substantial dish, but a bed of dressed salad leaves is all that is really necessary. This also makes an excellent light lunch for two.

SERVES 4

FOR THE MARINADE

- 3 Tbsp extra virgin olive oil
- 1 garlic clove, crushed
- 1 Tbsp chopped fresh rosemary
- 1 tsp balsamic vinegar
- Salt and ground black pepper

- 3 x 2-cm/¾-in slices orange pumpkin, seeded and peeled
- 6 rashers back bacon
- 18 small tomatoes (baby plums are ideal)
- 2–3 Tbsp freshly grated Parmesan cheese
- Dressed salad leaves, to serve

Preparation: 45 minutes
Cooking time: 8–10 minutes

❶ Mix all the ingredients for the marinade together in a shallow dish. Cut the pumpkin into 1-cm/½-inch pieces, then add to the dish, tossing it in the marinade. Leave for at least 30 minutes.

❷ Preheat the grill. Stretch the bacon, then cut the rashers in half lengthways, and roll them up. Thread the pumpkin, bacon and tomatoes onto thin metal skewers, then brush with any remaining marinade. Grill for 6 to 8 minutes, turning occasionally, until the pumpkin is tender and the bacon is browned.

❸ Scatter the grated cheese over the skewers as soon as they are cooked, so that it melts.

❹ Serve the skewers on a bed of dressed salad leaves.

Roast Crown Prince Squash and Pistachio Pâté

This really is one of my favourite recipes for squash. I don't miss meat, liver or fish in this thick pâté because the flavour and texture of the squash is wonderful. And it's so easy to make!

SERVES 6

- 675 g/1½ lb crown prince squash, seeded
- Salt and ground black pepper
- Olive oil
- 225 g/8 oz cream cheese
- 1–2 garlic cloves, crushed
- 1 hot red chilli, seeded and chopped fine
- 40 g/1½ oz pistachios, chopped

Preparation: 1½ hours
Chilling time: 30 minutes
---

❶ Preheat a 220°C/425°F/gas mark 7 oven. Cut the squash into 2.5-cm/ 1-inch slices. Place them in a roasting tin, and season lightly. Drizzle with olive oil, then roast for 45 minutes. Leave to cool, cut flesh from the skin and mash roughly.

❷ Beat the cream cheese with the garlic and chilli until smooth. Add the squash, mix together, then add the nuts and season well. Turn into a serving dish and chill for 30 minutes.

❸ Serve piled on hot toasts with a garnish of rocket leaves.

Curried Lamb and Pumpkin Koftas

Koftas are a cross between meatballs and kebabs, a meat mixture moulded onto skewers and then barbecued or grilled. I often mould the same mixture into baby patties and grill them, as this saves time.

Serves 4

- 1 onion, chopped
- 1 garlic clove
- 1 Tbsp curry powder
- 1–2 red chillies, chopped (optional)
- 1 green pepper, seeded and chopped
- 1 Tbsp oil or ghee
- 500 g/1 lb 2 oz minced lamb
- 225 g/8 oz thick pumpkin purée, fresh or canned
- Salt
- 75 g/3 oz fresh wholemeal breadcrumbs
- Oil, for cooking

Preparation: 25–30 minutes
Cooking time: 10 minutes

❶ Blend the onion, garlic, curry powder, chillies and pepper in a blender or food processor until smooth.

❷ Heat the oil in a large frying pan, add the lamb and cook quickly until browned all over, stirring frequently to break up any lumps of meat that form. Add the onion paste, cook for 2 to 3 minutes, then stir in the pumpkin and cook until it is heated through. Season to taste with the salt.

❸ Remove the pan from the heat and stir in the breadcrumbs to give a slightly moist but mouldable mixture. Allow to cool, then shape into 12 to 15 patties or mould around wooden skewers. Grill the koftas for 3 to 4 minutes on each side, brushing them from time to time with a little oil if necessary to keep them moist.

❹ Serve with a spoonful of rice or some salad leaves, and a yogurt dip—the cucumber and radish raita on page 34 would be ideal.

soups, starters & relishes

Spiced Minted Melon Balls

A spiced vinaigrette is the perfect foil for the sweetness of a melon that you wish to serve as a starter. Serve at room temperature and not chilled—too cold, and the melon will have little flavour, even if really ripe.

SERVES 4

- ½ tsp cumin seeds
- ½ ripe melon, such as cantaloupe, Galia or honeydew
- ½ medium cucumber, peeled and finely diced
- 3 tomatoes, seeded and diced
- 3 Tbsp finely chopped fresh mint
- Salt and sugar
- 3 Tbsp light olive oil
- 1 Tbsp white wine vinegar
- Mint sprigs, to garnish

Preparation: 30 minutes
Marinating time: 30 minutes

❶ Heat a small frying pan over medium heat, add the cumin seeds and toast them for just 30 seconds, until fragrant. Turn out of the pan and allow the seeds to cool.

❷ Scoop the melon into balls and place them in a bowl with the cucumber and tomatoes. Sprinkle the chopped mint with a little salt and sugar to bring out its flavour.

❸ Whisk together the oil, vinegar and mint. Grind the cumin seeds using a pestle and mortar or with the end of a rolling pin, then add them to the dressing, with salt and sugar to taste. Pour the dressing over the salad and leave to stand for 30 minutes. Serve in small dishes, garnished with sprigs of mint.

Pumpkin Chutney

If you buy a pumpkin in October to make chutney in December or January, do turn the pumpkin every day or so, to stop moisture collecting inside.

MAKES ABOUT 1.4 KG/3 LB

- 1 kg/2¼ lb prepared pumpkin flesh, diced
- 2 onions, finely chopped
- 1 Tbsp salt, plus 2 tsp
- 500 g/1 lb 2 oz fresh tomatoes, skinned, and chopped
- 100 g/4 oz sultanas
- 350 g/12 oz light soft brown sugar
- 1½ Tbsp ground ginger
- 2 garlic cloves, crushed
- 350 ml/12 fl oz white wine or distilled malt vinegar

Preparation: 15 minutes
+ 2 hours standing
Cooking time: 1 hour

❶ Mix the pumpkin and onion together, then add 1 tablespoon salt, stir well and leave for 2 hours. Drain and rinse well.

❷ Turn into a large preserving pan and add the remaining ingredients. Bring slowly to the boil, stirring all the time, then simmer for about 45 minutes, until reduced and thickened.

❸ Spoon into warm screw-top jars. Store for a month or more.

soups, starters & relishes

Pumpkin Chutney

Butternut and Chicken Liver Pâté

Meat or liver only pâtés can make a very rich prelude to a meal. Mix some garlic-flavoured livers with roasted butternut squash, and the resulting pâté is lighter and, even better, it goes further too! Using low-fat cream cheese helps to keep the calories and the richness of the pâté under control.

SERVES 6–8

- 1 butternut squash (weighing about 675–800 g/1½–1¾ lb)
- Salt and ground black pepper
- Olive oil
- 1 small onion, finely chopped
- 1 garlic clove, crushed
- 400 g/14 oz chicken livers
- 1 Tbsp fresh thyme leaves
- 225 g/8 oz low-fat cream cheese
- Thyme, paprika or melted butter, to garnish

Preparation and cooking time:
1 hour
Chilling time: 2 hours
---

❶ Preheat a 220°C/425°F/gas mark 7 oven. Cut the squash in half lengthways, scoop out the seeds, then arrange the halves in a small roasting tin. Season lightly, then drizzle with olive oil. Roast for 30 to 35 minutes, until the flesh is tender, then leave to cool.

❷ Heat 3 tablespoons of olive oil in a large frying pan, then add the onion and cook for 3 to 4 minutes until starting to soften. Add the garlic and chicken livers with the thyme, then cook over high heat for 3 to 4 minutes, until the livers are cooked through and lightly browned. Remove the pan from the heat and allow to cool.

❸ Scrape the cream cheese into the bowl of a blender or food processor and add the chicken liver mixture with the flesh of the butternut squash. Blend until smooth, then add seasonings to taste.

❹ Scrape the pâté into a serving bowl and smooth the top. Chill for 2 hours, then garnish with a sprig of thyme or paprika before serving. You could seal the top of the pâté with melted butter if you wish, which you should then allow to set for 30 minutes in the refrigerator. Serve the pâté with lots of fresh toast and a salad garnish, if you wish.

Pumpkin Relish

This Norwegian recipe keeps well and is utterly delicious—a surprising mixture of sweet and savoury.

MAKES 1.5–1.75 KG/3–4 LB.

- ½ medium orange pumpkin
- About 500 ml/18 fl oz white wine vinegar
- About 500 ml/18 fl oz water

Preparation: 20 minutes or overnight

Cooking time: 1 hour 15 minutes

---

❶ Seed and peel the pumpkin, then cut the flesh into 1-cm/½-inch dice.

Place in a large bowl, cover with equal parts white wine vinegar and water, then cover and leave for 8 hours or overnight.

❷ Drain the pumpkin and then weigh it. To each 1 kg/2¼ lb pumpkin, add 1 kg/2¼ lb sugar, 250 ml/9 fl oz white wine vinegar, 40 g/1½ oz chopped fresh root ginger.

❸ Mix the ingredients together in a large preserving pan, then bring slowly to the boil. Boil gently for 30 to 40 minutes, until the pumpkin is just soft, then scoop it out of the pan with a slotted spoon and pack into warmed glass jars. Pour over the slightly reduced syrup, then seal the jars loosely. Check the relish after 4 or 5 hours, then seal properly. Keep in a cool place and leave for a few weeks before eating.

Cucumber and Radish Raita

Cucumber raita has saved my palate several times when a curry has turned out hotter than planned!

SERVES 4 AS AN ACCOMPANIMENT

- 1 Tbsp white mustard seeds
- 1 Tbsp cumin seeds
- ½ medium cucumber
- 50 g/2 oz radishes, finely chopped
- 250 ml/9 fl oz natural yogurt
- Salt and ground black pepper
- 2 Tbsp chopped fresh coriander
- Chilli powder, to garnish

Preparation: 10 minutes

---

❶ Heat a frying pan over medium heat until hot, add the mustard and cumin seeds, and fry for not more than 1 minute, until the spices are fragrant and starting to brown. Turn out into a mortar or on to a chopping board and allow to cool slightly, then crush the seeds with a pestle or the end of a rolling pin.

❷ Grate the cucumber coarsely— this is easiest to do in a blender or food processor—then squeeze the

strands dry in your hands. Turn into a bowl, then add the spices, radishes and yogurt. Mix well, adding seasonings to taste, then add the coriander.

❸ Sprinkle the raita with chilli powder just before serving—not too much, though, as this is meant to be cooling, after all! (For a picture of this recipe, see page 105, Pumpkin and Okra Curry.)

soups, starters & relishes

Roasted Pumpkin, Tomato and Aubergine Salad

Roast Squash, Vegetable and Pasta Salad

Melon, Grape and Chicken Salad

Cucumber Salad with Spiced Pork and Sesame Seeds

Pasta Salad Verde

Warm Roasted Pumpkin and Green Bean Salad

Warm Mushroom and Patty Pan Salad

Gem Squash Salad

Chicory, Tomato and Melon Salad

Roasted Pepper and Squash Salad

Spiced Courgette and Roast Squash Salad

Squash, Cucumber and Bulgur Wheat Salad

Chilli Bean and Pumpkin Salad

Courgette and Squash Ratatouille with Melon

Pumpkin and Spinach Salad with Feta Cheese

Salads

35

Roast Pumpkin, Tomato and Aubergine Salad

Complementary flavours that pack a punch! Serve this salad warm or cold, on a bed of rocket leaves, with plenty of Italian flat bread.

SERVES 4

- 8 slices from a small pumpkin, each about 2-cm/¾-in thick, seeded
- 1 aubergine, quartered lengthways
- 2 large Marmande tomatoes, halved
- 6–8 elephant garlic cloves, unpeeled
- Salt and ground black pepper
- 6–8 basil leaves, torn in half
- Sugar
- Olive oil
- Basil leaves, to garnish
- Olive oil bread, to serve

FOR THE DRESSING

- 6 Tbsp extra virgin olive oil
- 1 Tbsp balsamic or sherry vinegar
- 1 tsp Dijon mustard
- Pinch of sugar
- 1 tsp chopped fresh young lovage leaves or 1 Tbsp chopped fresh flat leafed parsley

Preparation: 20 minutes
Cooking time: 45 minutes

❶ Preheat a 220°C/425°F/gas mark 7 oven. Arrange the prepared vegetables with the garlic in a roasting tin, then season with salt and pepper. Push the basil leaves into the flesh of the tomatoes, then scatter over a little sugar. Drizzle everything with olive oil, then roast at the top of the oven for 40–45 minutes, until the vegetables are just starting to blacken. (Check after 30 minutes and remove the tomatoes if they are already soft.)

❷ Allow the vegetables to cool slightly, then cut the pumpkin away from the skin. Leave for 10 minutes, if you intend to serve the salad warm, or until completely cold.

❸ Prepare the dressing by blending all the ingredients together and season with salt, pepper and sugar to taste.

❹ Peel the garlic, then arrange the vegetables on serving plates. Pour the dressing over and then add a little fresh basil to each helping. Serve immediately with plenty of olive oil bread.

salads

Roast Squash, Vegetable and Pasta Salad

A filling salad that you can enjoy either as a main course, or in smaller quantities as a starter.

SERVES 4 AS A MAIN COURSE,
6–8 AS A STARTER

- 4 x 2.5-cm/1-in slices crown prince squash, seeded
- 2 yellow courgettes, trimmed
- 1 large aubergine, halved lengthways
- 1 large red pepper
- 1 garlic bulb
- Salt and ground black pepper
- Olive oil
- 200 g/7 oz fresh or dried tagliatelli, spaghetti, or other noodles

FOR THE DRESSING
- 6 Tbsp extra virgin olive oil
- 2 Tbsp balsamic vinegar
- 1 tsp Dijon mustard
- Sugar
- Mixed salad leaves, to serve

Preparation: 30 minutes
Cooking time: 40 minutes

❶ Preheat a 220°C/425°F/gas mark 7 oven. Place all the vegetables in a roasting tin, season lightly and drizzle with olive oil. Roast for 40 minutes, or until they are tender and beginning to blacken. Turn the courgettes, red pepper and aubergine during cooking, and remove the vegetables as they are done.

❷ Cover the pepper with a damp cloth as soon as it comes out of the oven, then leave all the vegetables to cool. Peel the skin away from the pepper, then remove the core and seeds.

❸ Blend all the ingredients for the vinaigrette together and season well to taste. Cook the pasta, drain in a colander and shake briefly. Turn into a glass serving dish and add half the vinaigrette. Toss, then leave to cool completely.

❹ Peel the squash, then chop the roasted vegetables into bite-size pieces, and squeeze the garlic cloves from their skins. Pile the vegetables over the pasta, top with the salad leaves and pour over the remaining dressing. Toss just before serving.

Melon, Grape and Chicken Salad

A very filling salad comprising a wonderful mélange of ingredients. I like to use dolcelatte in the dressing, a slightly sweet cheese that draws out the flavours of the melon and grapes. Any crumbly blue would be a good alternative.

SERVES 2

- Mixed salad leaves
- 2 small cooked chicken breasts, skinned and boned
- ½ ripe melon, such as piel de sapo, Galia, cantaloupe or honeydew, scooped into balls
- 4 spring onions, chopped
- 2 tomatoes, seeded and chopped
- 1 mild red chilli, seeded and finely chopped
- ¼ medium cucumber, diced
- 50 g/2 oz small seedless black grapes
- Salt and ground black pepper

FOR THE DRESSING

- 3 Tbsp mayonnaise
- 50 g/2 oz blue cheese, crumbled
- Paprika, to garnish

Preparation: 15–20 minutes

❶ Arrange the salad leaves on two serving plates. Slice the chicken, then arrange on the leaves.

❷ Combine all the remaining salad ingredients and season well. Spoon over the chicken, drizzling any juices from the melon over the meat.

❸ Mix the mayonnaise with the crumbled cheese and season lightly, then dollop a spoonful of dressing on top of each portion.

❹ Sprinkle with paprika then serve immediately.

salads

39

Cucumber Salad with Spiced Pork and Sesame Seeds

A real main course of a salad, combining hot meat and vegetables with the crispness of salad leaves. The subtle spicing and the sesame seeds add extra interest.

SERVES 4
- 1 small head Chinese leaves, shredded
- 1 medium cucumber, seeded and diced
- 1 red pepper, seeded and sliced
- 3 Tbsp peanut oil
- 1 pork fillet (weighing about 500 g/1 lb 2 oz), trimmed and thinly sliced
- 1 tsp chilli sauce, or more according to taste
- 1 aubergine, thinly sliced
- 1 red onion, thinly sliced
- 1 garlic clove, sliced
- 1 green pepper, seeded and sliced
- 2 Tbsp light soy sauce
- 2 Tbsp sesame seeds

Preparation: 15 minutes
Cooking time: 10 minutes

---

❶ Arrange the leaves and cucumber in a large salad bowl with the red pepper, then leave in a cool place until required.

❷ Heat the oil in a large frying pan or wok, then add the pork fillet and cook quickly to brown. Add the chilli sauce, then the aubergine, and stir-fry until the aubergine is beginning to brown. Add the remaining vegetables and stir-fry briefly, then add the soy sauce. Scatter the sesame seeds into the pan, stir, then spoon the meat and vegetables over the prepared salad leaves. Toss lightly, then serve immediately.

Pasta Salad Verde

The secret of a really tasty salad is in the dressing. A healthy low-calorie vinaigrette simply will not do.

SERVES 4–6

- 250 g/9 oz tricoloured pasta shapes, such as fusilli
- 2 Tbsp extra virgin olive oil
- 4 large spring onions, finely chopped
- 2 courgettes, cut into julienne strips
- ½ medium cucumber, seeded and diced
- 75 g/3 oz spinach leaves, finely shredded

FOR THE DRESSING

- 1 large ripe avocado, peeled and chopped
- Juice of 1 lemon
- 100 ml/4 fl oz mayonnaise
- 100 ml/4 fl oz crème fraîche or natural yogurt
- 1 garlic clove, crushed
- 75 g/3 oz blue cheese, crumbled
- 1 mild green chilli, seeded and chopped

Preparation: 20 minutes
Cooking time: 15 minutes

❶ Bring a large pan of salted water to the boil, then add the pasta and cook according to instructions. Drain, then turn the pasta into a bowl and add the olive oil. Toss so that all the pasta is coated.

❷ Add all the prepared vegetables to the cold pasta, mix well and season. Mash the avocado with the lemon juice. Add the remaining dressing ingredients and blend well. Season to taste. Spoon on the dressing.

Warm Roasted Pumpkin and Green Bean Salad

A colourful combination that tastes really good! I like the contrasts between the vegetable shapes too.

SERVES 4

- 4 x 2.5 cm/1-in slices orange pumpkin, seeded
- Salt and ground black pepper
- Olive oil
- 1 large onion, finely chopped
- 1 garlic clove, finely sliced
- 400-g/14-oz can chopped tomatoes
- 250 g/9 oz green beans, cut into 2.5-cm/1-in lengths
- 8–10 fresh basil leaves, torn

Preparation: 1 hour
Cooking time: 15 minutes

❶ Preheat a 220°C/425°F/gas mark 7 oven. Place the pumpkin in a small roasting tin, season lightly and drizzle with olive oil. Roast the pumpkin for 40 to 45 minutes, or until tender.

❷ Meanwhile, prepare the sauce. Cook the onion in 2 tablespoons olive oil for about 5 minutes, until softened but not browned. Add the garlic and tomatoes, bring to the boil, then stir in the beans. Simmer for 8 to 10 minutes, until the beans are just tender, then season to taste.

❸ Peel the roasted pumpkin and cut into 2.5-cm/1-inch chunks. Add to the beans and tomatoes, then allow to cool slightly. Add the basil, then serve warm.

salads

Pumpkin and Spinach Salad with Feta Cheese

The soft texture and slightly sweet flavour of either pumpkin or squash combines very well with young spinach leaves, tomatoes and crumbly feta cheese to make a salad that will wake up your taste buds.

SERVES 4

- 3 Tbsp pine nuts
- 4 good handfuls young spinach leaves
- 75 g/3 oz rocket leaves
- 2 large Marmande tomatoes, thinly sliced, or 24 baby plum or cherry tomatoes
- 200 g/7 oz cooked pumpkin, diced
- 175 g/6 oz feta cheese, diced
- Salt and ground black pepper
- Extra virgin olive oil

Preparation: 10 minutes

---

❶ Heat a frying pan until hot, then add the pine nuts and stir-fry for 1 to 2 minutes, until lightly golden. Scoop the nuts out of the pan and leave to cool.

❷ Arrange the spinach and rocket leaves on a serving platter or individual plates, then top with the tomatoes, squash and cheese. Scatter the toasted pine nuts over, then season the salad lightly with salt and pepper.

❸ Drizzle with the olive oil just before serving.

TIP

The pumpkin and feta cheese should both be cut into equal-size diced chunks.

salads

Prawn and Courgette Lasagne

Squash with Prawns

Crab, Almond and Pumpkin Curry

Roast Monkfish and Pumpkin with Rice

Courgette and Fresh Tuna Risotto

Spicy Pumpkin Stuffed Cod

Grilled Sardines with Spaghetti Marrow

Hot Chilli Haddock with Spaghetti Marrow

Pumpkin Plaice with Courgette Sauce

Mixed Fish Cakes with Courgette Salad

Fisherman's Pumpkin Pie

Mussels and Squash with Tomato Spaghetti

Squash and Courgette Trout

Grilled Mackerel with Apple and Cucumber Salsa

Scallops with Baby Patty Pans and Bacon

Squid and Pumpkin Stew with Tomatoes

Fish Dishes

Prawn and Courgette Lasagne

I add lots of grated raw courgette to this lasagne before cooking, which gives a good texture to the dish. Leave the tomato sauce quite wet as the pasta will need the extra moisture to cook tender.

SERVES 4

- 1 onion, finely chopped
- 2 Tbsp olive oil
- 1 garlic clove, crushed
- 1 Tbsp fresh thyme leaves
- 100 ml/4 fl oz dry white wine
- 400-g/14-oz can chopped tomatoes
- Salt and ground black pepper
- 350 g/12 oz courgettes, grated
- 400 g/14 oz large peeled prawns
- 450 g/1 lb fromage frais
- 75 g/3 oz goat's cheese, with or without herbs, crumbled
- 10–12 sheets fresh no-cook lasagne

Preparation: 30 minutes
Cooking time: 30 minutes

---

❶ Preheat a 200°C/400°F/gas mark 6 oven. Lightly butter a suitably sized ovenproof gratin dish.

❷ Cook the onion in the oil until softened but not browned, then add the garlic and thyme. Add the wine, then cook quickly until it has almost evaporated. Stir in the chopped tomatoes, with some seasoning, then stir in the courgettes and prawns.

❸ Beat the fromage frais and goat's cheese together, and add a little seasoning to taste.

❹ Spoon half the courgette and prawn mixture into the buttered dish, then cover with a layer of lasagne. Repeat the layers, then finish by spooning the cheese mixture over the top.

❺ Bake the lasagne for 30 minutes, or until the topping is golden brown. Serve immediately.

fish dishes

54

Squash with Prawns

This recipe has long been a favourite of mine, and is one that I adapted from an idea for sweet potatoes. The smoked bacon and squash give wonderful background flavours to the garlic-fried prawns. Serve the dish with a little plain boiled rice—the squash is starchy, so you won't need much extra carbohydrate—and a large, crisp green salad or plenty of steamed vegetables.

SERVES 4

- 700 g/1 lb 9 oz prepared crown prince squash, cut into 2.5-cm/1-in chunks
- 5 Tbsp extra virgin olive oil
- 4 rashers smoked back bacon, diced
- 300 ml/½ pint vegetable stock
- 3–4 sprigs fresh thyme
- 2 bay leaves
- Salt and ground black pepper
- 50 g/2 oz butter
- 20 large unpeeled prawns, raw or cooked
- 1–2 plump garlic cloves, crushed
- 3 Tbsp white wine vinegar
- Fresh thyme leaves, to garnish

Preparation: 15 minutes
Cooking time: 30 minutes

❶ Cook the squash in the oil in a large frying pan for about 10 minutes, until starting to soften and brown, adding the diced bacon after 5 minutes. Then add the stock, herbs and seasoning, and bring to the boil. Cover and cook for 10 to 15 minutes, until the squash is just tender, then remove herbs.

❷ In a separate frying pan, melt the butter, add the prawns and garlic, and toss. Cook for 2 to 3 minutes until the prawns are hot, or until cooked through.

❸ Add the prawns and their juices to the squash with the vinegar, toss gently over the heat, and adjust the seasoning if necessary. Serve immediately, garnished with fresh thyme leaves.

fish dishes

Crab, Almond and Pumpkin Curry

A rich, mild curry to serve on a very special occasion. Increase the spiciness if you wish by adding a chopped chilli or two, but do not drown out the flavour of the crab and squash. Use a mixture of white and brown meats for the best flavour, or canned white crab meat if you prefer. Serve the curry with rice, or Indian flat breads.

SERVES 4

- 1 onion, chopped
- 1–2 garlic cloves, chopped
- 5-cm/2-in piece fresh root ginger, peeled and chopped
- 1 Tbsp mild curry powder
- 3 Tbsp groundnut oil
- 3 Tbsp whole blanched almonds
- 150 g/5 oz prepared pumpkin, diced
- 175 ml/6 fl oz milk
- 150 ml/¼ pint single cream
- 300 g/11 oz prepared crab meat
- Salt
- 2–3 Tbsp chopped fresh coriander

Preparation: 15 minutes
Cooking time: 12–15 minutes

❶ Blend the onion, garlic, ginger and curry powder until smooth in a blender or food processor. Heat the oil in a large frying pan, add the almonds and cook for 2 to 3 minutes, until golden brown. Scoop the nuts out of the oil with a slotted spoon and set aside.

❷ Add the diced pumpkin to the oil and cook over medium-high heat for 3 to 4 minutes, until starting to soften and brown, then add the curry paste. Lower the heat and cook for 5 minutes, stirring frequently.

❸ Stir the milk and cream into the curry, then add the crab meat with the almonds. Season lightly with salt, then heat gently until the crab meat is piping hot. Stir in the coriander and serve immediately.

Roast Monkfish and Pumpkin with Rice

Instead of serving this dish on a bed of rice, use it as a filling for flour tortillas for a change. Both ideas are equally delicious.

SERVES 4

- 20 x 2.5-cm/1-in dice (225g/8oz) prepared pumpkin
- 8 large tomatoes, halved
- 2 garlic cloves
- 1 small onion, quartered
- 2 mild red chillies, halved and seeded
- 3–4 large sprigs fresh basil
- 3–4 sprigs fresh oregano
- Salt and ground black pepper
- Sugar
- Olive oil
- 1 large monkfish tail (weighing 500–600 g/1 lb 2 oz–1 lb 5 oz)
- 275 g/10 oz easy-cook long grain rice
- Fresh basil sprigs, to garnish

Preparation: 15 minutes
Cooking time: 40 minutes
---

❶ Preheat a 220°C/425°F/gas mark 7 oven. Arrange the pumpkin at one end of a small roasting tin, the tomatoes, garlic, onion and chillies at the other. Tuck the fresh herbs amongst the tomatoes. Season all the vegetables, scatter the tomatoes with a little sugar, then drizzle everything with olive oil. Roast for 30 minutes, or until the pumpkin is tender and everything is just starting to blacken.

❷ Trim the monkfish tail and remove any skin. Season lightly, then place in a suitable baking dish and drizzle with olive oil. Roast with the vegetables for 15 to 20 minutes, until just cooked.

❸ Meanwhile, cook the rice according to the instructions.

❹ Remove the pumpkin from the roasting tin. To make the coulis, blend the remaining vegetables in a blender or food processor. Press the resulting paste through a sieve with the back of a ladle, then season according to taste.

❺ Strain the rice, if necessary, and arrange on four warmed plates. Cut the monkfish fillets away from the bone, then slice the fish thickly. Arrange the monkfish with the pumpkin over the rice, then spoon the coulis over. Garnish with the fresh basil and serve with steamed green vegetables or a tossed green salad, if you wish.

Courgette and Fresh Tuna Risotto

When there is a glut of courgettes in the garden we often make a risotto or spaghetti dish flavoured with just courgette, garlic and fresh Parmesan cheese. However, some fresh tuna, marinated in lime, olive oil and garlic, will turn a very simple dish into a splendid feast.

SERVES 4

- 500 g/1 lb 2 oz fresh tuna, cut into 2.5-cm/1-in dice
- Grated rind and juice of 2 limes
- 2 garlic cloves, crushed
- 6 Tbsp olive oil
- Salt and ground black pepper
- 1 large onion, chopped fine
- 250 g/9 oz arborio rice
- 1.2 litres/2 pints well-flavored fish or vegetable stock
- 500 g/1 lb 2 oz courgettes, grated
- Shavings of fresh Parmesan cheese, to garnish

Preparation: 10 minutes
+ marinating time
Cooking time: 25 minutes

---

❶ Place the tuna in a suitable glass dish, then add the grated lime rind and juice, 1 garlic clove and 3 tablespoons olive oil, with a little seasoning. Stir well, then cover and leave in a cool place for at least 1 hour, or up to a day. (If you leave the fish for around 24 hours, it will be almost pickled, and require very little cooking.)

❷ Cook the onion in the remaining oil in a large frying pan for 4 to 5 minutes, until soft but not browned. Add the rice and toss it in the pan juices, then stir in about one third of the stock. Bring to the boil, then cook until all the stock has been absorbed, stirring frequently. Add half the remaining stock and repeat the cooking process.

❸ Add the tuna and its marinade to the pan, and cook for 2 to 3 minutes, then add the remaining stock, and continue as before. Stir the grated courgette into the pan with the remaining garlic for the last 2 to 3 minutes of the cooking time, when the stock has almost all been absorbed.

❹ Season the risotto to taste, then serve with a tomato salad, if you wish, garnishing the risotto with shavings of fresh Parmesan cheese.

TIP
The easiest and most efficient way to shred courgette is in a blender or food processor.

fish dishes

Spicy Pumpkin Stuffed Cod

You will need really fresh cod fillet for this recipe, so that the flavour of the fish is not overpowered by the strength of the filling. I like to serve the roasted cod on the Chicory, Tomato and Melon Salad on page 44. The combination of spicy and sweet is just heavenly.

SERVES 4

- 4 thick pieces of cod fillet (weighing about 175 g/6 oz each) skinned
- 2 hot red chillies, seeded and finely chopped
- 2 garlic cloves, crushed
- 2 Tbsp chopped stoned black olives
- 4 Tbsp thick pumpkin purée, fresh or canned
- Salt and ground black pepper
- 3 Tbsp groundnut oil
- Knob of butter

Preparation: 10 minutes

Cooking time: 12–15 minutes

❶ Preheat a 220°C/425°F/gas mark 7 oven if you are intending to roast the cod. You could pan-fry the fish if you prefer, but roasting is easier.

❷ Prepare the cod fillets. Make a deep slit with a sharp knife along the top of each fillet—not quite to the ends—to make a pocket for stuffing. Mix together the chillies, garlic, olives and pumpkin, then season well with salt and pepper. Divide the mixture among the prepared fillets.

❸ Heat the oil with the butter in a large frying pan and brown the cod quickly on both sides. Reduce the heat and continue to cook the cod for 4 to 5 minutes on each side, or transfer it to a buttered baking sheet and roast, stuffing side up, for 6 to 8 minutes. Serve immediately.

Grilled Sardines with Spaghetti Squash

Really fresh sardines have a delicious flavour which doesn't want to be challenged by anything else. I have chosen a spaghetti squash to serve with them, but have diced it finely, and added chopped tomato and olives, along with a little olive oil—simple and delicious—rather than boiling it and scooping into strands. Pan-fry the sardines if you prefer, but grilling or barbecuing is best.

SERVES 4

- 1 small spaghetti squash (weighing about 750 g/1 lb 10 oz), peeled, seeded and cut into 1-cm/½-in dice
- 2 Tbsp extra virgin olive oil
- Knob of butter
- 12 fresh sardines, scaled
- 2 large tomatoes, seeded and diced
- 12 black olives, stoned and diced
- Salt and ground black pepper
- Green salad, to serve

Preparation: 10 minutes

Cooking time: 10 minutes

---

❶ Preheat the grill. Cook the diced squash in the oil and butter for 3 to 4 minutes, stirring frequently, while grilling the sardines for 2 to 3 minutes on each side. Brush the fish with a little oil before cooking, just to stop them sticking to the grill rack or pan.

❷ Toss the tomatoes and olives into the pan with the squash and just heat through. Season well, then pile the squash mixture onto warmed serving plates. Add the grilled sardines, a little green salad and serve immediately.

Hot Chilli Haddock with Spaghetti Squash

Spaghetti squash makes an unusual, slightly sweet garnish as it comes away in strands and deep-fries well. For best results, leave the parboiled squash for several hours to dry, so that the strands separate and do not stick together in the hot fat. I like to serve it with battered haddock which is spicily seasoned with a strong chilli sauce.

SERVES 3

- ½ small spaghetti squash
- 500 g/1 lb 2 oz piece thick haddock fillet, skinned and cut into thirds
- 2 Tbsp seasoned flour

FOR THE HOT CHILLI BATTER

- 100 g/4 oz plain flour
- 2 tsp hot chilli sauce
- 3 Tbsp sunflower or groundnut oil
- 250 ml/9 fl oz bitter beer
- 1 egg white
- Sunflower oil, for deep-frying
- Lemon wedges, to serve

**Preparation: 20 minutes
+ up to 4 hours drying time
Cooking time: 10 minutes**

---

❶ Cut the squash in half lengthways and scoop out the seeds. Bring one half to the boil in a pan of salted water, then simmer for 5 minutes. Drain upside-down and leave until cool enough to handle.

❷ Holding the shell upside-down over a baking sheet lined with absorbent kitchen paper, tease out the flesh using a fork. It will come out in strands like spaghetti. Let it fall loosely onto the baking sheet, then leave in a warm kitchen for about 4 hours to dry, or dry in a 150°C/300°F/gas mark 2 oven for 1½ to 2 hours, checking the squash regularly.

❸ Meanwhile, prepare the batter. Beat the flour, chilli sauce, oil and beer together until smooth. Leave to stand until required.

❹ Heat the oil to 180°C/355°F. Beat the egg white until stiff, then fold into the batter just before cooking the fish. Dip the prepared fish in the batter, then gently drop into the oil. Fry for 5 minutes, or until the batter is golden brown and crisp. Drain on plenty of crumpled absorbent kitchen paper. Sprinkle the squash with the seasoned flour, then drop it carefully, a little at a time, into the oil. Fry for just a few seconds until crisp, then remove from the pan with a slotted spoon and drain well.

❺ Serve the fish, garnished with the deep-fried squash and lemon wedges, for squeezing over.

Pumpkin Plaice with Courgette Sauce

I love plaice at lunch time—it is light, summery and not too filling. Mixed with pumpkin it becomes the perfect dish for early autumn eating—a little more substantial and comforting, but unlikely to send you off to sleep.

SERVES 2

- 2 plaice fillets (weighing about 175 g/6 oz each)
- Salt and white pepper
- 1 Tbsp groundnut oil
- Knob of butter
- 100 g/4 oz cooked pumpkin, diced
- 2 Tbsp fresh wholemeal breadcrumbs
- 2 Tbsp grated cheese, such as mozzarella or Cheddar cheese
- 3 spring onions, sliced
- 1 courgette, finely sliced
- 100 ml/4 fl oz single cream
- 2 Tbsp chopped fresh parsley

Preparation: 10 minutes
Cooking time: 12 minutes

❶ Preheat a 220°C/425°F/gas mark 7 oven. Season the plaice fillets lightly on both sides. Heat the oil and butter together in a large frying pan, then add the fillets, skin side up, and brown quickly. Transfer the fillets carefully to a buttered baking sheet.

❷ Mix together the pumpkin, breadcrumbs and cheese. Top the plaice fillets with the pumpkin mixture.

❸ Bake in the oven for 4 to 5 minutes or grill for the same amount of time, until the cheese is melting, the topping has set, and the fish is just cooked.

❹ Add a little more oil to the frying pan if necessary, then stir in the spring onions and courgettes, and cook for 3 to 4 minutes.

❺ Add the cream and heat until almost bubbling. Blend the sauce until smooth—this is easiest to do with a hand-held blender, but transfer the sauce to a blender or food processor if you wish. Season to taste, then serve the sauce spooned over the fish fillets, garnished with the chopped parsley.

fish dishes

Mixed Fish Cakes with Courgette Salad

These fish cakes are really light and delicious, and balance a raw vegetable salad very well. Use young, sweet courgettes, and if they are very small add an extra one to the mix.

Serves 4

- 1 carrot, cut into thin batons
- 2 courgettes, cut into thin batons
- 4 spring onions, finely chopped
- 2 tomatoes, seeded and chopped
- 1 mild chilli, finely chopped
- 2 Tbsp fish sauce
- 1 Tbsp light soy sauce
- Juice of 1 lemon

For the fish cakes

- 100 g/4 oz fresh breadcrumbs, white or wholemeal
- Milk
- 4 large spring onions, finely sliced
- 1 Tbsp groundnut oil
- 250 g/9 oz salmon fillet, skinned and cut into 5-mm/¼-in dice
- 250 g/9 oz hoki fillet, skinned and cut into 5-mm/¼-in dice
- 75 g/3 oz courgettes, grated
- Salt and ground black pepper
- 2–3 Tbsp mayonnaise

For the coating

- 50 g/2 oz ground almonds
- 75 g/3 oz fresh breadcrumbs, white or wholemeal
- ½–1 Tbsp groundnut oil, for frying

Preparation: 30–40 minutes
Cooking time: 10 minutes

❶ Combine all the salad ingredients, then leave to stand while preparing the fish cakes.

❷ For the fish cakes, soak the breadcrumbs in a little milk for a few minutes, then squeeze dry and discard the milk. Cook the spring onions in the oil in a large frying pan until soft but not browned. Mix with the breadcrumbs in a large bowl.

❸ Mix the diced fish with the breadcrumbs and all the remaining fish cake ingredients, adding just enough mayonnaise to bind the mixture.

❹ For the coating, mix the breadcrumbs and almonds together. Shape the fish mixture into 8 large fish cakes, coating them in the almond crumbs. Press the crumbs into the cakes.

❺ Heat some groundnut oil in the frying pan, then add the fish cakes and fry them gently for 4 to 5 minutes on each side. Serve the fish cakes on a bed of the courgette salad with some of the salad juices.

TIP

Ideally, use one green and one yellow courgette for the salad.

fish dishes

Fisherman's Pumpkin Pie

Use a selection of fish for this pie, but avoid smoked fillets which would dominate the dish. Keep it uncomplicated, and enjoy the flavours of the simple ingredients. Add a few peeled prawns if you wish.

SERVES 4

- 4 spring onions, finely sliced
- 3 Tbsp groundnut oil
- 350 g/12 oz prepared pumpkin, diced
- 700 g/1 lb 9 oz mixed white fish fillets, skinned and cut into 1-cm/½-in pieces
- 150 ml/¼ pint crème fraîche or soured cream
- Salt and white pepper
- 2 Tbsp chopped fresh parsley
- 10–12 sheets filo pastry
- 50 g/2 oz butter, melted

Preparation: 20 minutes
Cooking time: 40 minutes

❶ Preheat a 190°C/375°F/gas mark 5 oven. Lightly butter a deep, 20-cm/8-inch sandwich tin.

❷ Cook the spring onions in the oil in a large frying pan for about 2 to 3 minutes—do not let them brown—then add the pumpkin and cook gently for 4 to 5 minutes more, until the squash is just starting to soften. Take the pan off the heat, then stir in the fish, crème fraîche or soured cream and some seasoning with the chopped parsley. Set the filling aside.

❸ Arrange six or seven sheets of filo pastry in the base of the cake tin, draping them over the sides. Brush each sheet with butter, as you use it, to keep it moist and pliable. Pile the filling into the lined tin, then cover it with the remaining sheets of pastry, brushing them with butter as you go.

❹ Roll the edges of the pastry together, then fold them into the tin over the lid of the pie. Brush with any remaining butter and score the pastry lid deeply with a sharp serrated knife into diamonds.

❺ Bake for 30 to 40 minutes, until the pastry is crisp and golden brown. Serve immediately, with a green salad, if you wish.

TIP

When working with filo pastry, place it under a damp tea towel and only take the sheets out as you need them. This prevents them from becoming brittle.

Mussels and Squash with Tomato Spaghetti

Pasta has always been associated with shellfish—prawns, mussels, clams and cockles all go well with the thinner, flatter shapes such as spaghetti and tagliatelle. Add some squash and the fish goes further, making a more economical dish.

SERVES 4

- 350 g/12 oz dried spaghetti
- 1 large onion, finely chopped
- 3 Tbsp extra virgin olive oil
- 250 g/9 oz prepared butternut squash, diced
- 1 garlic clove, crushed
- 400-g/14-oz can chopped tomatoes
- Salt and ground black pepper
- 250 g/9 oz shelled mussels
- 10–12 torn fresh basil leaves

Preparation: 10 minutes

Cooking time: 20 minutes

---

❶ Bring a very large pan of salted water to the boil, then add the spaghetti and cook for 15 minutes, or according to the instructions on the packet.

❷ While the water is coming to the boil, cook the onion in the oil for 3 to 4 minutes in a large frying pan, until softened but not browned, then add the squash and cook for 2 to 3 minutes more. Stir in the garlic and tomatoes, with some salt and pepper, then simmer the sauce for 10 minutes, until slightly thickened. Stir in the mussels and cook for 2 to 3 minutes, until piping hot. Season well and add the basil.

❸ Drain the spaghetti and shake it briefly until dry. Add it to the frying pan (or pour the sauce over the spaghetti in the pasta pan if your frying pan isn't big enough) and toss the sauce and pasta together. Mound on to warmed plates and serve immediately.

Squash and Courgette Trout

Trout are such versatile fish and yet they are so often just served with almonds and slightly burnt butter. A mixture of squash and courgette complements the oily fish well, and I finish the dish with a fruity orange sauce.

SERVES 4

- 40 g/1½ oz butter, plus extra
- 1 Tbsp olive oil, plus extra
- 1 courgette, finely diced
- 200 g/7 oz cooked squash, such as crown prince, diced
- 4 rainbow or brown trout, about 250–275 g/9–10 oz each
- Grated rind and juice of 2 oranges
- 3 kaffir lime leaves, finely shredded
- 1–2 Tbsp crème fraîche
- Salt and ground black pepper

Preparation: 15 minutes

Cooking time: 25 minutes

---

❶ Heat the butter and oil together in a large frying pan, then add the diced courgette and squash. Cook for 3 to 4 minutes, until lightly browned, then scoop the vegetables out of the pan into an ovenproof dish and keep warm.

❷ Add a little extra butter and oil to the pan, then add the trout and fry gently for 5 to 6 minutes on each side. You might have to cook just two at a time. Transfer them to a plate and keep warm in a very low oven while finishing the sauce.

❸ Return the courgette and squash to the pan with the orange juice and shredded lime leaves. Cook for 1 to 2 minutes, then add the crème fraîche.

❹ Cook gently until the crème fraîche has heated through, add the orange rind and season. Serve the sauce spooned over the fish.

Grilled Mackerel with Apple and Cucumber Salsa

Mackerel is a very underrated fish. It is a rich source of the cholesterol-busting omega-3 oils, and is well partnered by a spicy apple and cucumber salsa.

SERVES 4

FOR THE SALSA

- 1 Tbsp white mustard seeds
- 2 tart red eating apples, cored and diced
- ½ medium cucumber, diced
- Grated rind and juice of 1 lemon
- 1 carrot, diced
- 1 hot red chilli, seeded and finely chopped
- 2 fresh tomatoes, seeded and diced
- 1 Tbsp white wine vinegar
- Salt and ground black pepper

- 8 fresh mackerel fillets
- 1 Tbsp medium oatmeal

Preparation: 45 minutes
Cooking time: 10 minutes

❶ Heat a frying pan, then add the mustard seeds and fry them for less than 1 minute, until really fragrant. Turn into a bowl and add all the ingredients for the salsa. Leave for 20 to 30 minutes, to allow the flavours to blend.

❷ Preheat the grill. Cover the grill pan rack with lightly oiled foil to make cooking and cleaning up easier. Season the mackerel fillets lightly, then grill skin side up for 3 to 4 minutes, depending on size. Turn the fillets carefully and grill for a further 3 to 4 minutes, until almost cooked.

❸ Scatter the oatmeal over the fish and cook for 1 to 2 minutes more, until lightly browned.

❹ Serve the mackerel with plenty of salsa and some freshly boiled potatoes, tossed in butter and chopped parsley, if you wish.

TIP

The apples, cucumber, carrot and tomatoes should be cut into even-size dice—about 5 mm/¼ inch thick.

fish dishes

Scallops with Baby Patty Pans and Bacon

I have always enjoyed scallops cooked with bacon—the two flavours are very complementary. I have chosen to include a recipe for this winning combination that is quick, easy and comes with its own sauce. Black spaghetti coloured with squid ink looks stunning to serve.

SERVES 3–4

- 250 g/9 oz baby patty pan squash, topped, tailed and halved horizontally
- 6 rashers streaky bacon, rinded and chopped
- 2 Tbsp extra virgin olive oil
- 450 g/1 lb scallops, sliced horizontally
- 2 garlic cloves, finely sliced
- 6 spring onions, finely sliced
- 150 ml/5 fl oz dry white wine
- 150 ml/¼ pint single cream
- Salt and white pepper
- 1–2 Tbsp freshly chopped parsley
- 225–275g/8–10oz black spaghetti
- Paprika, to garnish

Preparation: 10 minutes
Cooking time: 25 minutes

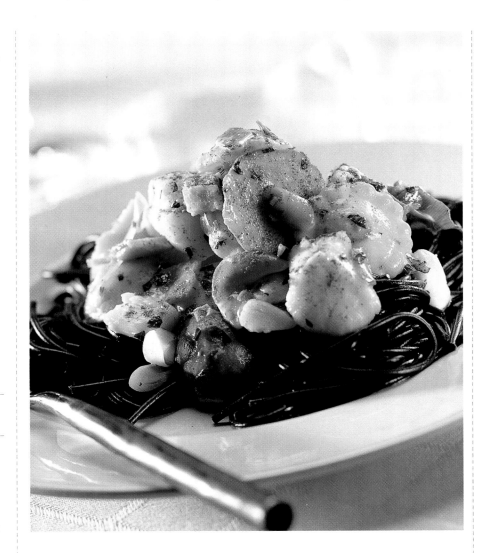

❶ Cook the squash and bacon in the oil over medium heat until the squash are just starting to soften—about 3 minutes—stirring frequently.

❷ Add the scallops and cook quickly for 30 to 60 seconds on each side, until they are a bold white colour, then add the garlic, spring onions and wine. Bring to the boil, scraping up any bits from the base of the pan, add the cream and season.

❸ Continue cooking briefly, for just 1 to 2 minutes, until all the ingredients are piping hot. Stir in the chopped parsley.

❹ To serve: drain the cooked black spaghetti and mould into nests in the centre of warmed serving plates. Spoon the scallops and squash into the nests, then spoon the sauce over. Sprinkle with paprika and serve immediately.

fish dishes

Squid and Pumpkin Stew with Tomatoes

So many people are put off squid when they have it badly fried and chewy. It should either be cooked very briefly, or stewed for a long time. This serves as a soup or main meal.

SERVES 4

- 1 large onion, finely chopped
- 3 Tbsp extra virgin olive oil
- 400 g/14 oz prepared pumpkin, diced
- 450 g/1 lb prepared squid rings
- 2 garlic cloves, finely sliced
- 2 tsp paprika
- 500 ml/18 fl oz passata or thick tomato juice
- 250 ml/9 fl oz fish or vegetable stock
- 2 bay leaves
- Salt and ground black pepper
- single cream and chopped fresh parsley, to garnish

Preparation: 20 minutes
Cooking time: 2 hours

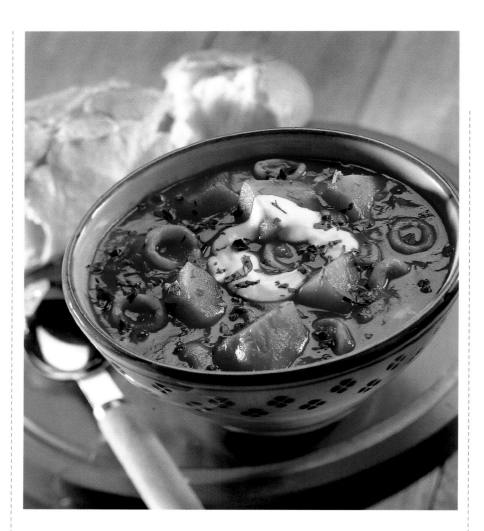

❶ Cook the onion for 5 to 6 minutes in the oil in a large pan over low heat, until softened but not browned. Add the pumpkin, continue to cook for 3 to 4 minutes, then stir in the squid. Increase the heat and cook for 2 to 3 minutes, until the squid is opaque, then add the garlic and paprika. Lower the heat and continue cooking for a further 2 to 3 minutes.

❷ Add the passata or tomato juice, the stock and bay leaves. Season well, then bring the stew slowly to the boil. Cover, and cook over very low heat for 1½–2 hours, stirring occasionally.

❸ Remove the bay leaves, then adjust the seasoning if necessary. Add a little water if the stew has become too thick.

❹ Serve in warmed bowls with a swirl of cream and a scattering of freshly chopped parsley.

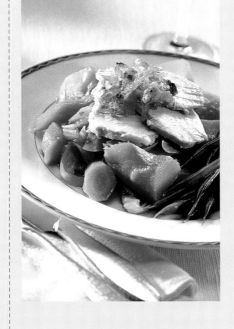

Lamb and Pumpkin Moussaka

Mexican Chilli with Spicy Squash

Spiced Lamb with Pumpkin and Chick Peas

Roast Lamb with Butternut Squash

Beef, Squash and Mustard Pie

Spiced Beef and Squash Stew with Cous Cous

Rich Daube of Beef with Baby Patty Pan Squash

Roast Sausage and Squash with Red Cabbage

Kabocha and Celery Stuffed Ham Rolls

Normandy Pork Fillet with Apples and Squash

Pot-roasted Pork with Squash

'Confit' of Duck with Gingered Pumpkin

Baked Onion Squash with Mexican Chicken

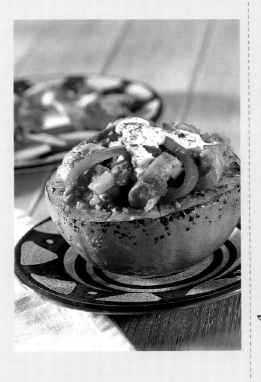

Red Rice Chicken Paella

Pumpkin Pizza with Chicken

Chicken and Courgette Sauce for Pasta

Turkey, Pumpkin and Cranberry Pie

Turkey and Squash Fricassée

Lamb and Pumpkin Moussaka

Moussaka is traditionally made with aubergine but it is actually rather good, for a change, with sliced pumpkin or squash. Try it—it's refreshingly different.

SERVES 6
- 1 large onion, finely chopped
- 2 Tbsp olive oil
- 500 g/1 lb 2 oz minced lamb
- 400-g/14-oz can chopped tomatoes
- 1 Tbsp tomato purée
- 1 garlic clove, crushed
- Salt and ground black pepper
- Freshly grated nutmeg
- 1 Tbsp chopped fresh oregano or marjoram
- 10–12 x 5-mm/¼-in slices pumpkin or squash, peeled and seeded

FOR THE TOPPING
- 250 ml/9 fl oz natural yogurt
- 250 ml/9 fl oz crème fraîche
- 100 g/4 oz soft goat's cheese, plain or with garlic and herbs

---
Preparation: 45 minutes
Cooking time: 50 minutes
---

❶ Cook the onion in the oil until soft but not browned, then add the minced lamb and cook over slightly higher heat until there is no pink meat left. Stir frequently to break up any lumps that form in the pan. Add all the remaining sauce ingredients, then bring to the boil. Simmer slowly for 30 minutes.

❷ Preheat a 190°C/375°F/gas mark 5 oven. The number of pumpkin or squash slices you will require will depend on the variety used. Layer the meat with the pumpkin or squash in a suitable buttered ovenproof dish, finishing with a layer of pumpkin or squash.

❸ Beat the yogurt, crème fraîche and goat's cheese together with some salt and pepper. Spread the mixture over the top of the moussaka. Place the dish on a baking sheet and cook in the oven for 45 to 50 minutes, or until the topping is browned and the squash is tender enough when a skewer is inserted into the centre of the dish.

❹ Leave to stand for a few minutes before serving with a tomato salad and fresh green leaves, or green vegetables, if you wish.

Mexican Chilli with Spicy Squash

Pan-fried, spicy, starchy squash is added to this chilli at the end of cooking instead of pinto or red kidney beans. The result is sweeter than the average chilli—and much more interesting.

SERVES 4

- 2 onions, chopped
- 2 tsp chilli powder, or to taste
- 1 tsp ground cumin
- 6 Tbsp groundnut oil
- 500 g/1 lb 2 oz minced lamb
- 1 Tbsp chopped fresh oregano
- 1 large cinnamon stick
- 2 garlic cloves, crushed
- 1–2 mild green chillies, seeded and chopped (optional)
- 400-g/14-oz can chopped tomatoes
- 1 Tbsp tomato purée
- Salt and ground black pepper
- 450 g/1 lb prepared squash, such as kabocha or crown prince, diced
- 1 tsp cumin seeds
- Soured cream and snipped fresh chives, to serve

Preparation: 10 minutes
Cooking time: 1½ hours or more

---

❶ Cook the onion with the chilli powder and ground cumin in half the oil over low heat for 4 to 5 minutes, until the onions are soft. Add the lamb, increase the heat slightly and cook until the lamb is well browned, then add the oregano, cinnamon and garlic. Add the chillies, if using, with the chopped tomatoes, tomato purée and seasoning, and stir well.

❷ Bring the chilli to the boil, then cover the pan and simmer slowly for at least 1 hour.

❸ Fry the squash in the remaining oil for 4 to 5 minutes, until browned and just soft, then add the cumin seeds and cook for 1 minute more. Add the squash to the chillies, then season again. Serve topped with a dollop of soured cream with fresh snipped chives scattered over. You could provide tortilla chips or garlic bread as an accompaniment.

Spiced Lamb with Pumpkin and Chick Peas

Heavy with Middle Eastern flavours, this spicy lamb stew can be made with either pumpkin or squash, but I think pumpkin works best as it is not quite so starchy with the chick peas. Serve with some sautéed potatoes and a tomato or green salad, or perhaps some green beans or courgettes.

SERVES 4

- 75 g/3 oz dried chick peas, soaked overnight
- 3 Tbsp olive oil, plus extra
- 225 g/8 oz lamb fillet, sliced
- 1 onion, finely sliced
- 500 g/1 lb 2 oz prepared pumpkin, diced
- 2 tsp ground cumin
- 1 tsp ground allspice
- 1 cinnamon stick, broken
- 150 ml/¼ pint red wine
- 400-g/14-oz can chopped tomatoes
- 350 ml/12 fl oz well-flavoured stock
- 100 g/4 oz ready-to-eat dried apricots
- Salt and ground black pepper
- 75 g/3 oz pistachios
- Chopped fresh coriander, to garnish

Preparation: 45 minutes and overnight soaking
Cooking time: 1 hour
---

❶ Drain the chick peas and rinse thoroughly under cold running water. Bring to the boil in a pan of fresh water, then cover and simmer for 30 to 40 minutes.

❷ Fry the lamb in the oil until browned on all sides, then remove from the pan with a slotted spoon, and set aside. Add the onion to the pan, cook over medium-high heat until lightly browned, then add the pumpkin and a little extra oil if necessary. Cook for 2 to 3 minutes, then stir in the spices, and continue cooking over low heat for another 1 to 2 minutes.

❸ Return the lamb fillet to the pan and add the wine. Bring to the boil, stirring all the time to scrape up any tasty bits from the base of the pan, then simmer until reduced by at least half. Stir in the tomatoes, stock and apricots, and add a little seasoning. Drain the chick peas, add them to the stew, cover and simmer for 30 minutes.

❹ Add the pistachios to the lamb and season to taste, removing the cinnamon stick. Serve garnished with chopped fresh coriander.

Roast Lamb with Butternut Squash

This is so simple, it's not really a recipe at all, but too delicious a combination of flavours to leave out of this book.

SERVES 6

- 1 leg of lamb (weighing 1.5–1.7 kg/3 lb 5 oz–3 lb 13 oz)
- 2 garlic cloves
- Salt and ground black pepper
- 1 butternut squash, quartered and seeded

Preparation: 5 minutes

Cooking time: about 2 hours

❶ Everyone has their favourite method of roasting lamb, so you can cook this quickly or slowly, whichever you prefer. Remember the squash will need about 45 minutes in a hot oven or around 1 hour at a more moderate temperature. Always allow 20 minutes for the joint to stand before carving, and build this into your schedule.

❷ Preheat a 200°C/400°F/gas mark 6 oven. Place the lamb in a roasting tin. Make some deep slits in the lamb and fill them with slivers of garlic. Calculate the roasting time by allowing 55 minutes per 1 kg/2¼ lb —just under 2 hours for this size leg of lamb. Season and roast for 1¼ hours.

❸ Add the squash to the roasting tin and baste with the meat juices. Roast for 30 minutes, remove the

lamb and wrap in foil. Continue roasting the squash until tender.

❹ Carve the lamb and serve the slices with the squash, and vegetables of your choice.

TIP

Instead of using slivers of garlic to stud the lamb, try sprigs of rosemary or pieces of anchovy instead.

meat and poultry

Beef, Squash and Mustard Pie

My Mum's steak and kidney pie was always one of my favourite dishes as a child. I have long since given up trying to make that particular dish as well as she does, but this pie which teams the beef with a firm winter squash is a good alternative. You could simmer the beef slowly on top of the cooker if you prefer.

SERVES 6

- 1 large onion, finely sliced
- 2 Tbsp oil
- 500 g/1 lb 2 oz braising steak, trimmed and cut into bite-size pieces
- 2 Tbsp dark soy sauce
- 2 star anise
- Ground black pepper
- 450 ml/¾ pint light bitter beer, plus extra if needed
- 4 x 2.5-cm/1-in slices (350g/12oz) crown prince squash
- 2 Tbsp whole grain mustard
- 225 g/8 oz ready-made puff pastry

**Preparation: 30 minutes
Cooking time: 4 hours and
40 minutes**

❶ Preheat a 160°C/325°F/gas mark 3 oven. Cook the onion in the oil over medium-high heat until just starting to brown, then add the beef and continue cooking until both are well browned on all sides. Transfer the meat to a casserole or pie dish, add the soy sauce and bury the star anise in the meat. Season well.

❷ Add the beer to the pan and bring to the boil, stirring all the time to scrape up any sediment. Pour the beer over the meat, adding a little extra as necessary just to cover the meat. Cover the casserole and cook in the oven for 2½–3 hours, or until the beef is tender. Allow to cool.

❸ Reheat the oven to 220°C/425°F/ gas mark 7. Place the squash in a roasting tin, then season lightly and drizzle with oil. Roast the squash for 40 minutes, or until tender. Leave to cool for 10 to 15 minutes. Lower the oven temperature to 200°C/ 400°F/gas mark 6.

❹ Trim away the skin from the squash and chop the flesh into 2.5-cm/1-inch dice. Stir the squash into the beef with the mustard.

❺ Roll out the pastry and use to cover the beef and squash. Use any trimmings to decorate the pie, then bake for 35 to 40 minutes, until the pastry is golden brown.

TIP

I often cook the meat in advance and leave it to cool completely before covering with the pastry.

Spiced Beef and Squash Stew with Cous Cous

Flavoured with cumin and chilli, two widely used spices in northern Africa, this stew is served with a mound of cous cous in the middle of each helping in large, dished plates. It makes a satisfying meal.

SERVES 4

- 3 Tbsp olive oil
- 500 g/1 lb 2 oz chuck steak, cut into 2.5-cm/1-in pieces
- 1 large onion, finely sliced
- 2 tsp mild chilli powder
- 2 tsp ground cumin
- 1 large cinnamon stick
- 1–2 hot red chillies, seeded, if liked, and finely chopped
- 700 g/1 lb 9 oz prepared winter squash, cut into 2.5-cm/1-in pieces
- 150 ml/¼ pint red wine
- 2 courgettes, diced
- 2 garlic cloves
- 400-g/14-oz can chopped tomatoes
- 600 ml/1 pint well-flavoured stock
- Salt and ground black pepper
- 175 g/6 oz cous cous

Preparation: 30 minutes

Cooking time: 2½ hours

---

❶ Preheat a 160°C/325°F/gas mark 3 oven. Heat the oil in a flameproof casserole, brown the beef, then remove it from the pan.

❷ Add the onion to the casserole, cook quickly until well browned but not burnt, then add the spices and chillies with the squash. Continue to cook over low heat for 6 to 8 minutes, until the squash softens.

❸ Return the beef to the pan with the red wine and bring slowly to the boil, stirring all the time. Add the diced courgettes with the garlic, then the chopped tomatoes and sufficient stock to just cover the meat, about 350 ml/12 fl oz. Season well then bring the stew slowly to the boil. Cover, transfer to the oven and cook for 2 to 2½ hours.

❹ Just before the beef is ready, bring the remaining stock to the boil in a saucepan. Add the cous cous, then cover and leave, off the heat, for about 10 minutes, until the grains have absorbed the liquid and become fluffy. Moisten with a little olive oil if necessary, then serve with the beef.

TIP

You could serve this dish simply on a bed of green vegetables.

meat and poultry

Rich Daube of Beef with Baby Patty Pan Squash

A daube is a rich beef stew from the Burgundy region of France, traditionally seasoned with orange.

SERVES 6

- 900 g/2 lb blade bone braising steak, cut into 5-cm/2-in pieces
- 3 Tbsp extra virgin olive oil
- 1 large onion, sliced
- 225 g/8 oz streaky bacon, chopped
- 2 large carrots, thickly sliced
- 1 Tbsp red wine vinegar
- 3 large sprigs fresh thyme
- 1 large cinnamon stick, broken
- 4 bay leaves
- ½ tsp cloves
- 2–3 garlic cloves, finely sliced
- Grated rind of 1 large orange
- 1 bottle full-flavoured red wine
- 2 Tbsp tomato purée
- Salt and ground black pepper
- 500 g/1 lb 2 oz baby patty pan squash, topped and tailed
- 2 Tbsp chopped fresh parsley

Preparation: 20–25 minutes
Cooking time: 3¼ hours

❶ Preheat a 160°C/325°F/gas mark 3 oven. Cook the beef in the oil in a large flameproof frying pan over medium-high heat until well browned on both sides.

❷ Remove the beef from the pan and add the onion, bacon and carrots. Cook over low heat until the onions are tender and starting to brown. Add the vinegar and stir until all the sediment from the base of the pan has been scraped up.

❸ Return the beef to the pan, then add all the herbs and spices, garlic, orange rind, wine and tomato purée with some seasoning. Bring slowly to the boil, then cover the pan and transfer to the oven. Cook for 3 hours, or until the beef is tender.

❹ Trim the patty pans. Season the daube to taste, removing the bay leaves, cinnamon and twigs from the thyme, then add the squash. Cover and cook in the oven for 10 to 15 minutes more, or until the squash are just tender. Garnish with parsley, then serve with your choice of potatoes, rice or pasta.

meat and poultry

78

Roast Sausage and Squash with Red Cabbage

I have always loved sausages, especially high-quality, coarse-cut, prime meat varieties. The squash sweetens the cabbage well, and makes the sausages go further.

SERVES 4

- 8 thick sausages, pork, beef or venison
- 4 x 2.5-cm/1-in slices (350 g/12 oz) winter squash, such as Hubbard, crown prince or kabocha
- Salt and ground black pepper

FOR THE CABBAGE

- 1 large onion, finely chopped
- 1 Tbsp mustard seeds
- 3 Tbsp olive oil
- 300 g/11 oz red cabbage, shredded
- 1 Tbsp red wine vinegar
- 100 ml/4 fl oz red wine
- Salt and ground black pepper

Preparation: 10 minutes
Cooking time: 45 minutes
---

❶ Preheat a 200°C/400°F/gas mark 6 oven. Arrange the sausages and the squash in a roasting tin. Season the squash, then cook in the oven for 40 to 45 minutes.

❷ Cook the onion and the mustard seeds in the oil for 2 minutes, then add the cabbage and continue to cook for 2 minutes more. Stir in the vinegar and wine and seasonings, then cover the pan and simmer the cabbage for 30 minutes.

❸ Cut away the skin from the squash, then dice the flesh and stir it into the cabbage. Season to taste, then serve with the sausages.

TIP

Unless your sausages have natural skins, remember to prick them with a fork before cooking them in the oven, to prevent them from splitting.

meat and poultry

Kabocha and Celery Stuffed Ham Rolls

An unusual Thai-flavoured sweet-and-sour filling for creamy baked ham rolls. These would make a good starter before a light main course but also make an excellent lunch or supper dish.

SERVES 4

- 3 Tbsp groundnut oil
- 1 onion, finely sliced
- 400 g/14 oz prepared kabocha squash, diced
- 1 stalk lemon grass, bruised and finely chopped
- 3 sticks celery, chopped
- 1 red chilli, seeded and finely chopped (optional)
- 1 tsp tamarind paste
- 4 large slices of ham
- 2 kaffir lime leaves, finely shredded
- 300 ml/½ pint single cream
- Salt and ground black pepper

Preparation: 30 minutes

Cooking time: 20 minutes

---

❶ Heat the oil in a large frying pan, add the onion and cook until just starting to brown—do this over medium–high heat so that the onion softens as well.

❷ Add the squash with the lemon grass and celery, and continue to cook for 4 to 5 minutes before adding the chilli and tamarind paste. Stir well, then continue to cook slowly for about 15 minutes, until the squash is almost tender.

❸ Meanwhile, preheat a 190°C/375°F/gas mark 5 oven and lightly butter a suitable gratin dish. Divide the squash filling among the four slices of ham and roll up carefully. Spoon any leftover filling into the base of the dish, then arrange the ham rolls on top. Stir the lime leaves into the cream, season, then pour over the rolls into the dish.

❹ Bake for 20 minutes, until the cream is lightly browned. Serve immediately, with stir-fried vegetables and rice, if you wish.

TIP

Instead of cream, use coconut milk for the sauce. Or you could use a combination of the two.

Normandy Pork Fillet with Apples and Squash

This dish is based on the many traditional Normandy dishes of chicken or pheasant cooked with apples and calvados, the apple brandy of northern France.

SERVES 3–4

- 2 Tbsp olive oil, plus extra
- Knob of butter
- 1 gem squash, peeled, seeded and sliced
- 1 sharp green eating apple, cored and sliced
- 500 g/1 lb 2 oz pork fillet, trimmed and cut into 1-cm/½-in slices
- 1 onion, finely sliced
- 1 garlic clove, finely chopped
- 250 ml/9 fl oz dry cider
- Salt and ground black pepper
- 150 ml/1/4 pint calvados or brandy
- 2–3 Tbsp crème fraîche
- Chopped fresh parsley, to garnish

Preparation: 10 minutes

Cooking time: 30 minutes

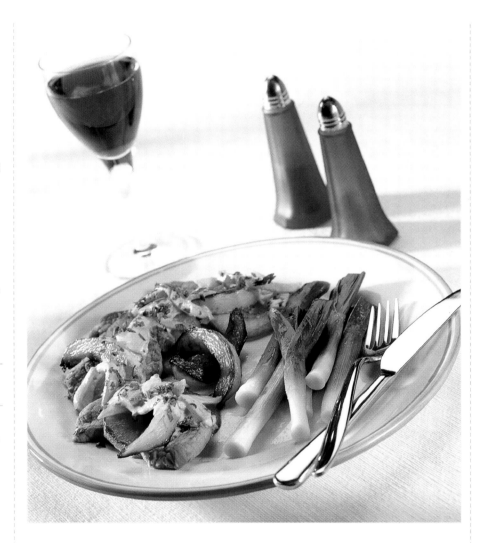

❶ Heat the oil and butter together in a large frying pan, then cook the squash until softened and browned on both sides. Remove with a slotted spoon, then repeat with the apple rings. Set aside with the squash.

❷ Add extra oil if necessary, then add the sliced pork and cook in the same way. Stir in the onion and cook until starting to brown. Add the garlic, cider and season. Bring to the boil, stirring to scrape up any sediment from the base of the pan, then simmer slowly for 15 minutes.

❸ Heat the calvados or brandy slowly until it ignites. Pour into the pork, off the heat. Leave until the flames subside.

❹ Stir the crème fraîche into the pan with the squash and apple. Heat gently until the cream has combined with the sauce, and the squash and apples are hot. Season to taste, then serve garnished with the chopped fresh parsley.

meat and poultry

Pot-roasted Pork with Squash

I have long enjoyed meat or poultry with fruit juices. Chicken and peaches is a favourite and somehow this very fragrant sauce with pot-roasted pork reminds me of it.

SERVES 6

- 1 joint sparerib of pork (weighing about 1.5 kg/3 lb 5 oz)
- 2 Tbsp groundnut oil
- 1 large onion, finely sliced
- 2 carrots, chopped
- 4 celery stalks, chopped
- 500 g/1 lb 2 oz prepared winter squash, such as crown prince or kabocha, chopped
- 1 garlic clove, crushed
- 1 Tbsp chopped fresh lovage, or 3 Tbsp chopped fresh flat-leafed parsley
- 2–3 blades mace
- Salt and ground black pepper
- 300 ml/½ pint well-flavoured vegetable or chicken stock

Preparation: 15–20 minutes

Cooking time: 2½ hours

---

❶ Preheat a 160°C/325°F/gas mark 3 oven. Brown the pork in the oil in a heavy flameproof casserole over high heat. Remove from the pan.

❷ Toss all vegetables, except the garlic, in the oily juices. Cook over medium heat until they begin to soften. Add the garlic, lovage or parsley, and the mace, then arrange the meat in the pan on the vegetables.

❸ Pour the stock into the pan and bring slowly to the boil. Cover, then cook in the oven for at least 2 hours, preferably 2½ hours, until the pork is tender. Lift the meat from the pan, wrap in foil and leave to rest for 15 minutes before carving. If you wish, you could cut the crackling off the joint at this stage and cook it under

the grill until crispy. Chopped up, it makes a contrasting garnish.

❹ Blend the vegetables and pan juices to a thick sauce and season well. Use a hand-held blender or blend in a blender or food processor. Carve the pork and serve it with the sauce spooned over.

'Confit' of Duck with Gingered Pumpkin

I love confit but I have always felt that it must take ages to prepare, and be a very sticky, greasy job to accomplish. Well, this quick way of doing it may not be wholly authentic, but it is very rich, delicious and easy. It is also a good dish for entertaining, as the duckling benefits from being cooked a day in advance. I use pumpkin rather than squash as it is softer and blends into the noodles more easily.

SERVES 4

- 4 duckling leg portions
- Chicken fat
- 150 ml/¼ pint water
- Groundnut oil
- 4 x 2.5-cm/1-in slices (350 g/12 oz) of pumpkin, seeded

FOR THE MARINADE

- 3 Tbsp chopped fresh root ginger
- 2 large garlic cloves, crushed
- 1 Tbsp star anise
- 1 tsp ground white pepper
- 2 Tbsp coarse sea salt

- 50 g/2 oz dried thread egg noodles
- 8 spring onions, sliced diagonally
- 1 Tbsp white wine vinegar
- 5-cm/2-in piece fresh root ginger, coarsely shredded
- Fresh coriander, to garnish

Preparation: 1 hour, plus overnight marinating time
Cooking time: 1½ hours plus 1 hour

❶ Trim the duckling legs, removing any excess skin. Scrape any fat from the skin and chop roughly. Place the fat in a small pan with any chicken fat that you may have, and the water. Bring to the boil, then cover and simmer slowly for 45 minutes, or until all the fat is clear.

❷ Marinate the duckling in a dish by scattering the spices evenly over the portions. Use just enough salt to give a good covering to the top surface of the duck, then set aside. Leave to marinate for 1 hour minimum, preferably overnight.

❸ Preheat a 200°C/400°F/gas mark 6 oven. Rinse the duckling portions under cold running water to remove all the salt and spices, then pack into a casserole which will just take them snugly. Strain the fat mixture over the duckling legs, then add sufficient groundnut oil to cover the portions completely. Cover the dish and cook in the oven for 30 minutes, then reduce the heat to 160°C/325°F/gas mark 3, and cook for 1 hour more, or until the duckling is very tender but not falling off the bone. Leave to cool in the fat, preferably overnight.

❹ When cool or the next day, preheat a 220°C/425°F/gas mark 7 oven. Place the pumpkin in a roasting tin, season lightly and smear with a little of the fat from the marinated duckling. Cook in the oven for 30 minutes.

❺ Remove the duckling from the fat and scrape off the excess. Place the portions in the roasting tin with the pumpkin and cook for 20 to 25 minutes, turning once. Remove the pumpkin after 10 to 15 minutes, once tender, and turn the duckling. At the same time, strain off and reserve most of the fat. Leave sufficient to keep the meat moist and to prevent it from sticking to the tin.

❻ Meanwhile, cover the noodles with boiling water and leave to stand for 5 minutes before draining. Measure 2 tablespoons of the drained duck fat into a pan, add the spring onions and cook briefly. Add the vinegar, then squeeze the juice from the ginger shreds into the pan. Fork the pumpkin into strands, scraping it from the skin, and add it to the spring onions with the drained noodles. Season to taste.

❼ Make a small pile of pumpkin noodles on each of four warmed serving plates, then place a piece of confit on each. Spoon a little of the fat over, with any juices from the noodles, garnish with coriander, and serve immediately.

Baked Onion Squash with Mexican Chicken

Onion squash replaces flour tortillas as the holder for a spicy Mexican chicken filling, served topped with soured cream. This is a filling meal which requires only a small Mexican-style salad of lettuce, spring onions, tomato and avocado to accompany it.

SERVES 2

- 1 small onion squash (weighing about 800 g/1¾ lb)
- 25 g/1 oz butter
- 2 garlic cloves, crushed
- 1 hot red chilli, seeded and finely chopped
- 3 Tbsp groundnut oil
- 2 chicken breast fillets, skinned and diced
- 1 onion, finely chopped
- 1–2 tsp chilli powder
- 1 tsp ground cumin
- 1 green pepper, seeded and sliced
- 200 g/7 oz canned chopped tomatoes
- Salt and ground black pepper
- Soured cream, to serve

Preparation: 25 minutes
Cooking time: 30 minutes

❶ Preheat a 220°C/425°F/gas mark 7 oven. Top and tail the squash, then cut it in half horizontally. Scoop out the seeds and score the flesh in the two halves deeply before placing them in a small roasting tin or gratin dish. Melt the butter, stir in half the garlic and the chopped chilli, then brush the mixture over the squash, letting it trickle into the score marks. Roast the squash for 15 minutes or so, while preparing the filling.

❷ Heat the oil in a large frying pan, then add the diced chicken and cook until beginning to brown. Add the onion, remaining garlic and spices, then reduce the heat and continue to cook gently for 4 to 5 minutes, until the onion has softened. Stir from time to time to prevent the spices from burning.

❸ Add the pepper and tomatoes, and bring the mixture to the boil, stirring all the time to scrape up any sediment from the base of the pan.

❹ Season well, then pile the filling into the half-cooked squash shells. Cover loosely with foil, then return the squash to the oven for 15 minutes.

❺ Remove the foil, then continue to roast the filled squash for 10 to 15 minutes more, until the squash is tender and both the vegetable shells and the filling are starting to blacken. Serve immediately, topped with soured cream.

meat and poultry

86

Pumpkin Pizza with Chicken

This is a really novel pizza with a Mediterranean accent, using wonderfully unusual but complementary ingredients.

SERVES 3–4

- 350 g/12 oz strong white bread flour
- 2 tsp salt
- 1 Tbsp easy-blend dried yeast
- 3 Tbsp extra virgin olive oil
- 400-g/14-oz can pumpkin purée
- About 150 ml/¼ pint warm water
- 200 g/7 oz mozzarella cheese
- 1 large onion, finely sliced
- 225 g/8 oz cooked chicken breast, sliced
- 3 Tbsp small black olives
- 2 Tbsp capers
- Olive oil, for drizzling

Preparation: 1 hour
Cooking time: 25 minutes

---

❶ Mix the flour with the salt and dried yeast in a bowl, then add the oil, half the pumpkin purée and sufficient water to mix to a manageable bread dough. Knead thoroughly until smooth and elastic.

❷ Flour a large baking sheet. Roll the dough out to a circle about 38 cm/15 inches in diameter and lift it on to the baking sheet—it doesn't matter if it overlaps the sides of the baking sheet slightly at this stage.

❸ Shred half the mozzarella and scatter it around the edge of the dough. Damp the crust and fold it over the cheese, leaving a circle about 30 cm/12 inches in diameter. Cover with a damp cloth and leave the dough to rise for about 40 minutes.

❹ Preheat a 220°C/425°F/gas mark 7 oven. Spread the remaining pumpkin over the risen pizza base, then top with the sliced onion, chicken, olives and capers. Season well, then top with the remaining mozzarella, thinly sliced, and drizzle with a little olive oil.

❺ Bake for 20 to 25 minutes, until the crust is golden brown. Serve in wedges, with a tossed green salad if you wish.

meat and poultry

Chicken and Courgette Sauce for Pasta

Miniced chicken is now widely available in supermarkets. For a dish like this, which has a very rich tomato sauce, poultry is ideal as it is lower in fat than the more traditional beef or lamb.

SERVES 4

- 1 large onion, finely chopped
- 2 Tbsp extra virgin olive oil
- 500 g/1 lb 2 oz minced chicken
- 150 ml/¼ pint red wine
- 3 courgettes, diced
- 2 garlic cloves, crushed
- 4 halves sun-dried tomatoes in oil, shredded
- 100 g/4 oz mushrooms, sliced
- 400-g/14-oz can chopped tomatoes
- 1 Tbsp tomato purée
- 2 Tbsp chopped fresh oregano
- Salt and ground black pepper

Preparation: 10 minutes
Cooking time: From 45 minutes to 1¼–1½ hours, the longer the better

---

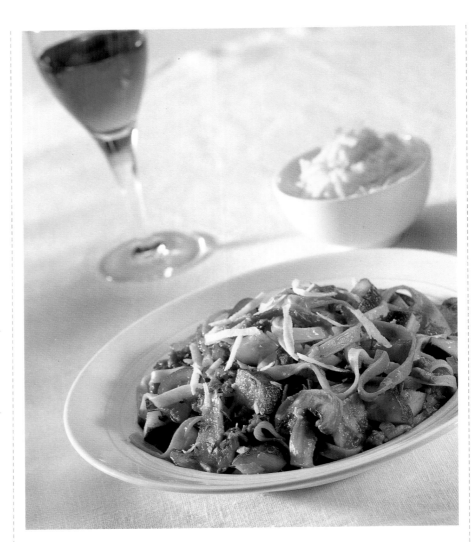

❶ Cook the onion in the oil over low heat until softened but not browned, then add the minced chicken and cook slightly more quickly, until no pink meat is left. Stir frequently to break up any lumps of meat that may form in the pan. Add the wine, then continue to cook over medium-high heat until reduced by at least one third.

❷ Add the remaining ingredients and season well with salt and pepper. Bring the sauce to the boil, then simmer slowly for at least 30 minutes—up to 1 hour is ideal.

❸ Season the sauce again before serving. Toss into freshly cooked pasta and sprinkle with Parmesan.

TIP

If you prefer, use minced turkey in this recipe. This resulting dish will be equally good.

meat and poultry

Turkey, Pumpkin and Cranberry Pie

Raised pies are brilliant for busy weekends when you cannot foresee time in the kitchen as they can be baked ahead. This pie is particularly moist—the cranberries cook down juicily, and the turkey and pumpkin are kept succulent by the fatty belly of pork.

SERVES 8

FOR THE HOT WATER CRUST PASTRY

- 350 g/12 oz plain flour
- 2 tsp salt
- 115 g/4½ oz lard
- 150 ml/¼ pint mixed milk and water

FOR THE FILLING

- 600 g/1 lb 5 oz boneless turkey breast, finely diced
- 400 g/14 oz belly of pork, rinded and finely chopped
- 250 g/9 oz prepared pumpkin, diced
- 250 g/9 oz fresh cranberries
- 5-cm/2-in piece fresh root ginger, grated and squeezed
- 1 tsp cardamom seeds, crushed
- Freshly grated nutmeg
- Grated rind and juice of 1 orange
- 1 tsp salt
- ½ tsp ground black pepper

- 1 large egg, beaten
- 1 Tbsp gelatine or aspic powder
- 250 ml/9 fl oz boiling water

Preparation: 45–50 minutes
Cooking time: 1½ hours

❶ Preheat a 200°C/400°F/gas mark 6 oven. For the pastry, mix the flour and salt in a large bowl and make a well in the centre. Melt the lard into the milk and water in a small pan, bring to the boil, then pour immediately into the flour. Mix to a soft, manageable dough, then turn onto the work surface and knead lightly until smooth. Cover the pastry with the upturned mixing bowl and leave to stand until cool enough to handle.

❷ For the filling, mix all the ingredients together, using about half a nutmeg for seasoning.

❸ Roll out two thirds of the pastry into a large circle and use to line a 23-cm/9-inch, 5-cm/2-inch deep springform tin. Press the pastry well into the corners and up the side of the tin. Pack in the filling, pressing it down firmly with the back of a spoon, then roll out the remaining pastry into a circular lid for the pie. Brush the edges of the pastry with egg, then press both crusts together, and seal. Use your fingers to press the pastry into a decorative edge. Make a small slit in the centre of the lid to allow the steam to escape.

❹ Add a pinch of salt to the beaten egg, and use to brush the lid of the pie. Set aside any remaining egg. Bake for about 1 hour then carefully run a knife between the side of the tin and the pastry. This will loosen the pie from the edge—meat juices may have escaped and made the pastry stick. Open the spring on the tin and remove the side. If the tin will not release the pie without tearing the pastry, return to the oven for 10 to 15 minutes more, then try again. Place the pie on a baking sheet and brush the sides and top with half the reserved beaten egg. Bake for 30 minutes more, brushing the pie again with egg after 15 minutes.

❺ Let the pie cool. Stir the gelatine or aspic into the hot water, then leave to dissolve completely. Cool slightly, but do not allow the mixture to set. Carefully pour the jelly mixture into the pie, through the slit in the lid, until you can force no more in. Chill the pie for at least 3 hours before slicing and serving.

Turkey and Squash Fricassée

If you are a real squash enthusiast like me, there will be times when you have a selection of leftovers in the vegetable basket. This is an ideal dish for using them up, along with any leftover turkey.

SERVES 4

- 3 Tbsp oil
- 6 spring onions, chopped
- 225 g/8 oz cooked chicken, diced
- 675 g/1½ lb prepared mixed winter squash, diced
- 100 ml/4 fl oz dry white wine
- 225 ml/8 fl oz soured cream
- Salt and ground black pepper
- Boiled rice, to serve
- Chopped fresh parsley, to garnish

Preparation: 10–15 minutes
Cooking time: 20 minutes

❶ Heat the oil in a large frying pan, add the spring onions and chicken, and cook quickly for 2 to 3 minutes, then add the squash. Toss to coat, then cover the pan and cook slowly for about 10 minutes, until the cubes of squash have softened.

❷ Pour the wine into the pan and cook quickly, stirring all the time, until reduced by half. Stir in the soured cream, season to taste, then heat gently without boiling.

❸ Serve on a bed of rice, garnished with chopped parsley.

TIP
If you wish, add a few mushrooms to this dish but make sure they are closed cup mushrooms so they do not discolour the fricassée.

Acorn Squash with Lentil and Celery Sauce

Spinach and Courgette Pie

Butternut Squash and Cauliflower Bake

Mediterranean Baked Stuffed Squash

Roast Pumpkin Ratatouille Cobbler

Curried Banana Squash

Squash Stuffed Roasted Peppers

Pumpkin and Haricot Bean Cassoulet

Baked Stuffed Patty Pan Squash

Blue Cheese and Pecan Risotto with Squash

Squash and Okra Curry

Savoury Country Pumpkin Pie

Kabocha, Fennel and Orange Casserole

Squash and Apricot Bulgur Risotto

Spiced Pumpkin Soufflé

Main Course Vegetable Dishes

Acorn Squash with Lentil and Celery Sauce

A relatively quick dish to cook, but one which is filling and full of flavour. I like to use a ridged grill pan to cook the squash, as the appearance is then so attractive, but an ordinary frying pan will cook it.

Serves 4

- 1 onion, chopped
- 4 sticks celery, chopped
- 3 Tbsp olive oil, plus extra
- 100 g/4 oz Puy or green lentils
- 100 ml/4 fl oz red wine
- 400-g/14-oz can chopped tomatoes
- 1–2 cloves garlic, crushed
- 4 large sprigs thyme
- 2 bay leaves
- 1 acorn squash, trimmed
- Salt and ground black pepper

Preparation: 10 minutes

Cooking time: 40 minutes

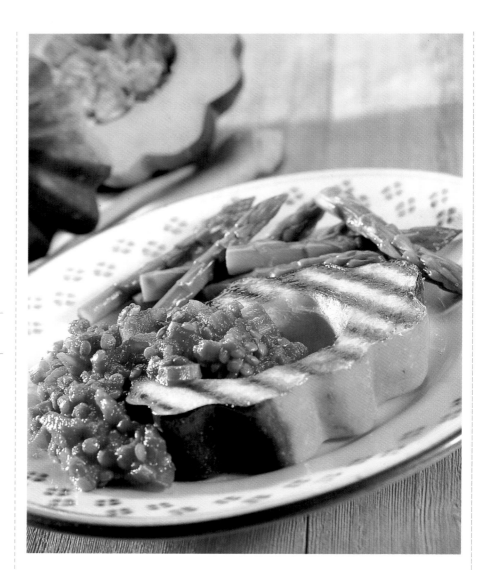

❶ Cook the onion and celery in the oil until softened but not browned, then add the lentils and wine. Simmer until the wine is slightly reduced, then add the chopped tomatoes, garlic and herbs. Bring to the boil, then simmer for 30 minutes, until the sauce has thickened and the lentils are tender.

❷ Cut the squash, unpeeled, into four thick rings and remove the seeds. Preheat a griddle pan or a large frying pan and add a little olive oil. Cook the squash for 5 minutes on each side over medium heat, pressing down firmly at first, to encourage the marking from the griddle if used. The squash rings may be kept warm in a medium oven if necessary.

❸ Season the sauce well with salt and pepper, then remove the thyme and bay leaves. Serve the sauce spooned over the squash rings, with freshly cooked green vegetables.

main course vegetable dishes

Spinach and Courgette Pie

A variation on the popular Greek spinach pie Spanakopitta. *The grated courgettes give it more body and texture.*

SERVES 6

- 1 large onion, chopped
- 2 Tbsp olive oil
- 400 g/14 oz courgettes, grated
- 300 g/11 oz fresh leaf spinach, shredded
- 2 garlic cloves, crushed
- 3 Tbsp pumpkin seeds
- Salt, ground black pepper and freshly grated nutmeg
- 200 g/7 oz cream cheese
- 12–15 sheets filo pastry
- 50 g/2 oz butter, melted

Preparation: 25 minutes

Cooking time 30 minutes

---

❶ Preheat a 200°C/400°F/gas mark 6 oven. Cook the onion in the olive oil until soft, then add the courgettes and stir-fry for 2 to 3 minutes.

❷ Add the chopped spinach (with just the water clinging to it after washing) with the garlic and continue to cook over high heat, stirring constantly, for 2 to 3 minutes, until the spinach has wilted and most of the water has evaporated.

❸ Remove the pan from the heat, add the pumpkin seeds and season well with salt, pepper and nutmeg.

Stir in the cream cheese, allowing it to melt over the hot vegetables.

❹ Line a deep 20-cm/8-inch sandwich tin, preferably with a removable base, with sheets of filo pastry, brushed with melted butter, letting them drape over the sides of the tin. The pastry will need to be about three sheets thick. Pile the filling into the pastry case, then cover with four or five sheets of filo. Roll the edges of the pastry case and lid together, folding them in over the pastry lid, then brush them well with more melted butter.

❺ Score the pastry topping into diamonds with a sharp knife, then bake the pie for 25 to 30 minutes, until the pastry is crisp and golden brown. Serve warm, cut into generous wedges.

TIP

Any filo pastry sheets left over can be wrapped in cling film and put in the freezer for later use.

main course vegetable dishes

Butternut Squash and Cauliflower Bake

This is more filling than a cauliflower cheese, and provides the ideal 'comfort food' dish.

SERVES 4

- 1 butternut squash (weighing about 1 kg/2¼ lb)
- 1 large onion, finely chopped
- 3 Tbsp olive oil
- 1–2 tsp sweet Spanish paprika
- 1 small cauliflower, weighing about 400 g/14 oz, cut into florets
- 2 x 400-g/14-oz cans chopped tomatoes
- 2 Tbsp chopped fresh tarragon
- 1 Tbsp caraway seeds (optional)
- 1–2 garlic cloves, finely sliced
- Salt and ground black pepper
- About 250 ml/9 fl oz well-flavoured vegetable stock
- 150 g/5 oz fresh wholemeal breadcrumbs
- 175 g/6 oz Cheddar cheese, grated

Preparation: 15 minutes

Cooking time: 1½ hours

❶ Preheat a 190°C/375°F/gas mark 5 oven. Cut the squash in half and remove the seeds, then peel away the skin with a sharp knife. Cut the flesh into roughly 2.5-cm/1-inch pieces.

❷ Cook the onion in the oil for 3 to 4 minutes in a flameproof casserole, then stir in the squash and paprika. Cook for 2 to 3 minutes more, then add the cauliflower, tomatoes, tarragon, caraway seeds, if using, garlic and seasoning. Add sufficient stock to almost cover the vegetables, then bring to the boil. Cover the casserole dish and cook in the oven for 1 hour.

❸ Mix together the breadcrumbs and cheese, then scatter the topping over the vegetables. Increase the oven temperature to 200°C/400°F/gas mark 6, then bake, uncovered, for 15 to 20 minutes more, until the topping has browned. Serve immediately, with fresh crusty bread and freshly cooked green vegetables if you like.

Mediterranean Baked Stuffed Squash

The sunshine flavours of the Mediterranean baked in a squash. This is a very satisfying dish.

SERVES 4

- 2 small squash, such as acorn or red kuri, weighing about 750 g/ 1 lb 10 oz each
- Salt and ground black pepper
- Olive oil

FOR THE FILLING

- 4 large spring onions, finely chopped
- 1 garlic clove, crushed
- 6 halves sun-dried tomatoes in oil, shredded
- 1 small courgette, trimmed and cut into 5-mm/¼-in dice
- 1 small yellow courgette, trimmed and cut into 5-mm/¼-in dice
- 10 large green olives, stoned and chopped
- 65 g/2½ oz fresh wholemeal breadcrumbs
- 2 Tbsp chopped fresh parsley
- 2–3 Tbsp oil from the tomatoes or melted butter

Preparation: 15 minutes

Cooking time: 25 minutes

---

❶ Preheat a 220°C/425°F/gas mark 7 oven. Cut the squash in half and scoop out the seeds, then trim the base of each piece so that the shells will sit flat. Place the shells, cut side up, in a large roasting tin. Season lightly, then drizzle with olive oil. Roast the squash for 10 minutes whilst preparing the filling.

❷ Mix all the ingredients for the filling together with plenty of seasoning. Bind together with oil or melted butter, then spoon into the part-roasted squash shells. Mound the filling in the shells, return to the oven and continue cooking for 20 to 25 minutes, until the filling is browned and the squash are tender.

❸ Serve immediately, with freshly cooked vegetables or a mixed salad.

Roast Pumpkin Ratatouille Cobbler

A great dish for hungry vegetarians and meat-eaters alike. The hot roasting oven used for the pumpkin is further employed to finish the dish, baking the cheese scone topping. Serve with freshly cooked vegetables of your choice.

SERVES 4–6

- 6 x 2.5-cm/1-in thick slices peeled, seeded pumpkin (weighing about 750 g/1 lb 10 oz)
- Salt and ground black pepper
- Olive oil
- 1 large onion, chopped
- 2 green peppers, sliced
- 1 aubergine, diced
- 2 courgettes, diced
- 1–2 garlic cloves, finely sliced
- 450 g/1 lb passata or thick tomato juice

FOR THE TOPPING

- 225 g/8 oz plain flour
- 1½ tsp baking powder
- 1 tsp mustard powder
- Pinch of salt
- 50 g/2 oz butter
- 75 g/3 oz Cheddar cheese, grated
- About 150 ml/¼ pint cold milk
- crème fraîche, to serve (optional)

Preparation: 1 hour
Cooking time: 20–25 minutes

❶ Preheat a 220°C/425°F/gas mark 7 oven. Arrange the pumpkin slices in a small roasting tin, season, then drizzle with olive oil. Roast for 40 to 45 minutes.

❷ Cook the onion in 3 tablespoons olive oil in an ovenproof casserole dish until soft, then add the peppers and aubergine. Toss the vegetables in the hot oil, then cook them slowly for 3 to 4 minutes. Stir in the diced courgettes and garlic, then add the passata or tomato juice. Season well, then bring slowly to the boil. Cover and simmer for 20 to 25 minutes, then season to taste.

❸ Remove the pumpkin from the oven and leave to stand until cool. Cut the flesh away from the skin and chop into 2.5-cm/1-inch dice. Add the pumpkin to the ratatouille and stir in any extra seasoning.

❹ Stir together flour, baking powder, mustard and salt, then blend in the butter until the mixture resembles fine breadcrumbs. Stir in the cheese, then mix to a soft but manageable

main course vegetable dishes

dough with the milk. Knead lightly on a floured surface, then roll into eight rough balls and drop into the top of the ratatouille.

❺ Bake for 18 to 20 minutes, until the scone topping is golden brown and well risen. Serve immediately, with a dollop of crème fraîche if using.

Curried Banana Squash

This curry is stir-fried, and simple and quick to prepare

SERVES 4

FOR THE CURRY PASTE

- 2 large onions, chopped
- 4 garlic cloves, chopped
- 5-cm/2-in piece fresh root ginger, peeled
- 1 hot red chilli, seeded and chopped
- 1–2 Tbsp curry powder
- 1 Tbsp tomato purée
- 1 tsp salt

- 100 g/4 oz blanched almonds
- 3 Tbsp groundnut oil
- 675 g/1½ lb prepared banana squash, diced
- 50 g/2 oz creamed coconut, crumbled
- 250 ml/9 fl oz water
- Salt and ground black pepper

Preparation: 10 minutes
Cooking time: 25 minutes

❶ Blend ingredients for the paste in a blender or food processor. Fry almonds until golden.

❷ Remove almonds and add the squash. Cook until it browns, then stir in the paste. Fry for 2 to 3 minutes, add the coconut and stir until melted.

❸ Add water, then bring to the boil. Simmer for 15 to 20 minutes. Before serving, add the almonds and warm through.

Squash Stuffed Roasted Peppers

Red peppers are much sweeter than green for baking or roasting; yellow are the next best.

SERVES 4

- 4 large red peppers
- 450 g/1 lb prepared firm-fleshed squash, such as crown prince, acorn or kabocha, diced
- 2 large garlic cloves, finely sliced
- Salt and ground black pepper
- 4 tomatoes, skinned, halved, seeded
- 300 ml/½ pint single cream
- 75 g/3 oz freshly grated Parmesan cheese
- Olive oil

Preparation: 15 minutes
Cooking time: 35 minutes

❶ Preheat a 220°C/425°F/gas mark 7 oven. Cut the peppers in half lengthways through the stalk. Take out core and seeds. Rinse and arrange in an ovenproof dish.

❷ Pile the diced squash into the peppers, burying the sliced garlic in amongst the pieces. Season well, then top with the halved tomatoes.

❸ Mix the cream with the Parmesan cheese and a little more seasoning, then carefully pour the mixture into the peppers.

❹ Drizzle a little olive oil over, then bake at the top of the hot oven for 30 to 35 minutes, until the peppers are starting to blacken and the cheese is browned.

❺ Serve hot, perhaps with a few salad leaves or stir-fried courgettes.

Pumpkin and Haricot Bean Cassoulet

A cassoulet is usually made with a variety of fatty meats such as goose, belly pork, ham and garlic sausage. This is a far healthier version of the classic French dish, but retains the texture and filling characteristics of the dish that it is modelled on.

SERVES 6

- 275 g/10 oz dried haricot beans, soaked overnight
- 2 large onions, sliced
- 3 Tbsp olive oil
- 500 g/1 lb 2 oz prepared pumpkin, diced
- 2 garlic cloves, sliced
- 3 courgettes, cut into 1-cm/½-in dice
- Salt and ground black pepper
- 400-g/14-oz can chopped tomatoes
- 4 large sprigs thyme
- 3 bay leaves
- 750 ml/1¼ pints well-flavoured vegetable stock
- 225 g/8 oz fresh wholemeal breadcrumbs

**Preparation: 1 hour
+ overnight soaking
Cooking time: 1½ hours**

❶ Drain the beans and rinse thoroughly in fresh, cold water. Bring to the boil in a large pan of fresh water, then cover, and simmer for 1 hour. Meanwhile, prepare the remaining ingredients.

❷ Preheat a 160°C/325°F/gas mark 3 oven. Cook the onions in the oil in a large flameproof casserole for 5 to 6 minutes, until soft but not browned. Add the prepared pumpkin and cook for 4 to 5 minutes more, then stir in the garlic and courgettes. Season well, then pour the chopped tomatoes over the vegetables.

❸ Drain the beans and place them in a thick layer over the vegetables, tucking the thyme and bay leaves into them. Add salt and pepper, and sufficient stock to come to just below the level of the beans. Cover the casserole and cook in the oven for 1 hour.

❹ Remove the lid of the casserole and take out the sprigs of thyme and the bay leaves. Make a thick layer of the breadcrumbs over the beans. Increase the oven temperature to 200°C/400°F/gas mark 6 and return the cassoulet to the oven for 20 minutes more, until the topping is browned and crisp.

Baked Stuffed Patty Pan Squash

Big patty pan squashes make excellent stuffed vegetables. They have a soft skin and do not require peeling and I sometimes think the flesh has a slight hint of coconut about it. I trim off the stalk of the squash, then turn it upside-down to cut a round out of the base to scoop out the seeds. I also cook and serve the squash upside-down, as I think it looks better that way!

SERVES 4

- 1 patty pan squash (weighing about 1 kg/2¼ lb)
- Salt and ground black pepper
- 3 Tbsp extra virgin olive oil
- 1 large onion, chopped fine
- 2 sticks celery, chopped
- 1 garlic clove
- 175 g/6 oz mushrooms, sliced
- ½ tsp ground mace
- 400-g/14-oz can chopped tomatoes
- 3 Tbsp chopped fresh parsley

Preparation: 30 minutes

Cooking time: 25 minutes

❶ Preheat a 200°C/400°F/gas mark 6 oven. Cut a circle from the base of the squash and scoop out the seeds. Season the cavity and trickle 1 tablespoon of oil around it. Bake the squash in a roasting tin for 20 minutes while preparing the filling.

❷ Cook the onion and celery in the remaining oil, in a large frying pan, for 4 to 5 minutes over low heat, until softened but not browned. Stir in the garlic and mushrooms, with the mace, and cook for 2 to 3 minutes more, until the mushrooms are soft and the juices run. Add the chopped tomatoes, with a little salt and pepper, then simmer for 10 minutes, until reduced and slightly thickened. Add extra salt and pepper to taste, then stir in the parsley.

❸ Spoon the tomato and mushroom filling into the part-baked squash, then bake for 20 to 25 minutes more, until the squash is tender. Serve cut into quarters, perhaps with a lentil salad and a green leaf salad.

Blue Cheese and Pecan Risotto with Squash

A brilliant risotto, and so unusual! I prefer to use a piquant blue cheese such as Stilton to give a tangy, sharp zing. However, a sweeter cheese, such as dolcelatte, will give a more subtle flavouring. The pecans are sweet and almost mystical in the slightly sticky rice.

SERVES 4

- Good pinch saffron threads
- 1.2 litres/2 pints well-flavoured vegetable stock
- 2 Tbsp olive oil
- Knob of butter
- 1 onion, finely chopped
- 250 g/9 oz prepared squash, such as crown prince, acorn or golden Hubbard, diced
- 2 garlic cloves, crushed
- 300 g/11 oz arborio rice
- 12 sage leaves, shredded
- 150 g/5 oz blue cheese, crumbled
- 100 g/4 oz pecans, chopped
- Salt and ground black pepper
- Dressed rocket leaves, to garnish

Preparation: 15 minutes
Cooking time: 30–40 minutes

❶ Soak the saffron in the almost boiling stock until required—keep the stock as warm as possible. Heat the oil and butter together in a large frying pan, then add the onion and cook over low heat until softened.

❷ Add the squash and cook quite quickly, until almost starting to brown. Stir in the garlic and the rice, and toss to coat in oil.

❸ Add one third of the stock, then bring the rice to the boil and cook, stirring frequently, until almost all the stock has been absorbed. Add half the remaining stock and repeat the cooking process, then add the sage leaves followed by the remaining stock. Continue cooking until most of the stock has been absorbed, then stir in the crumbled cheese and the pecans.

❹ Continue cooking until the cheese has just melted, then remove the pan from the heat and season the mixture well. Serve garnished.

TIP

Substitute walnuts for the pecans, if you wish, but only use 50 g/2 oz as their dominant flavour can easily overpower the dish.

main course vegetable dishes

104

Squash and Okra Curry

The secret with okra is to cook it for quite a long time, until the texture is somewhat sticky. Instead of banana squash, you could use acorn or golden Hubbard.

SERVES 3–4

FOR THE CURRY PASTE
- 1 large onion, chopped
- 2–3 garlic cloves, chopped
- 1 Tbsp curry powder
- 2 green chillies, seeded and chopped
- 2 Tbsp lime or prawn pickle
- 1 Tbsp brown sugar
- 1 tsp salt
- 1 Tbsp tomato purée

- 500 g/1 lb 2 oz prepared banana squash, diced
- 3 Tbsp groundnut oil, plus extra
- 450 g/1 lb okra, trimmed and cut into 1-cm/½-in slices
- 250 ml/9 fl oz water or vegetable stock
- 400-g/14-oz can chick peas, drained
- 2–3 Tbsp chopped fresh coriander
- Natural yogurt and rice or Indian flat breads, to serve

Preparation: 10 minutes
Cooking time: 1 hour

❶ Blend all the ingredients for the curry paste together in a blender or food processor. Add a little oil or water to make a smooth paste.

❷ Cook the squash in the oil in a large pan for 4 to 5 minutes, then add the okra. Sauté the vegetables together for 2 to 3 minutes.

❸ Scrape the curry paste into the pan, cook over low heat for 4 to 5 minutes, then add the water or stock. Bring to the boil, then simmer the curry for 40 minutes, until the squash and the okra are tender.

❹ Stir in the drained chick peas and cook for 5 minutes more. Adjust seasoning, add coriander and serve.

main course vegetable dishes

105

Savoury Country Pumpkin Pie

A simple vegetable pie, but one that is full of texture and flavour. Use as wide a selection of vegetables as you can; you could even use two or three varieties of squash which should make up about one third of the total. The capers add a touch of the exotic, and you could use a blue cheese, goat's cheese or Parmesan instead of Cheddar, if you prefer.

SERVES 4–5

- 1 kg/2¼ lb potatoes
- 1 kg/2¼ lb mixed vegetables, cut into 2.5-cm/1-in chunks, such as pumpkin, parsnips, carrots, onions, leeks and courgettes
- 3 Tbsp capers
- Salt and ground black pepper
- 900 ml/1½ pints milk
- 100 g/4 oz butter
- 4 Tbsp flour
- 100 g/4 oz Cheddar cheese, grated

Preparation: 35 minutes
Cooking time: 50 minutes

---

❶ Preheat a 190°C/375°F/gas mark 5 oven and butter a large gratin dish. Bring the potatoes to the boil in a large pan of salted water, simmer for 5 minutes. Drain and let cool.

❷ Bring another large pan of water to the boil, then add all the prepared vegetables. Return to the boil, then simmer for 10 minutes. Drain thoroughly in a colander, turn into the prepared dish and add the capers with some salt and pepper.

❸ Slice the potatoes and arrange them over the vegetables. Combine the milk, butter and flour in a pan and bring slowly to the boil, stirring all the time. Continue to cook the sauce for 1 minute, until thickened, then add the cheese and seasoning to taste. Pour the sauce over the potatoes and spread it evenly. Place the gratin dish on a baking sheet if it is very full.

❹ Bake the pie for 45 to 50 minutes, until the topping is well browned. Serve in generous portions, with freshly cooked green vegetables, such as broccoli, broad beans or French beans.

main course vegetable dishes

Kabocha, Fennel and Orange Casserole

I have always liked the combination of fennel and orange. Add some kabocha squash and you have a satisfying and tasty casserole to serve with brown rice.

SERVES 4

- 500 g/1 lb 2 oz prepared kabocha squash, cut into 2.5-cm/1-in pieces
- 4 Tbsp extra virgin olive oil
- 1 large onion, chopped
- 4 sticks celery, chopped
- 1 large fennel bulb, trimmed and finely sliced
- 100 g/4 oz Puy or green lentils
- 400-g/14-oz can chopped tomatoes
- 250 ml/9 fl oz well-flavoured vegetable stock
- Salt and ground black pepper
- 3 bay leaves
- 1 Tbsp chopped fresh sage
- Grated rind and chopped flesh of 2 oranges
- 100 g/4 oz pecans
- Cooked brown rice, to serve

Preparation: 15 minutes
Cooking time: 1 hour

❶ Cook the squash in the oil in a large saucepan until just starting to brown and soften. This will take about 4 to 5 minutes over medium-high heat. Stir in the onion, celery and fennel, reduce the heat and cook gently for 3 to 4 minutes.

❷ Add the lentils, tomatoes and stock with some seasoning, the bay leaves and sage. Bring to the boil, then simmer very gently for 30 to 40 minutes, until the squash is tender.

❸ Stir in the chopped orange and the nuts, and cook for 1 to 2 minutes more, just to heat through. Remove the bay leaves and adjust the seasoning if necessary. Serve the casserole on a bed of brown rice, garnished with the orange rind and any fronds from the fennel bulb.

TIP

The ideal garnish for this dish are the feathery fronds from the top of the fennel bulb.

Squash and Apricot Bulgur Risotto

The coarse grains of bulgur or cracked wheat make an excellent alternative to rice for this risotto, which has a very exciting combination of fruity flavours and vegetables.

SERVES 4

- 1 large onion, sliced
- 1 leek, trimmed and sliced
- 2 Tbsp olive oil
- 400 g/14 oz prepared squash, such as crown prince, diced
- 1 tsp ground cumin
- 1 tsp ground ginger
- 1–2 plump garlic cloves, finely sliced
- 4 sticks celery, sliced
- 1 red pepper, sliced
- 275 g/8 oz bulgur wheat
- 100 g/4 oz ready-to-eat dried apricots, chopped
- 400 g/14 oz chopped tomatoes
- 750 ml/1¼ pints water or stock
- Salt and ground black pepper
- 100 g/4 oz mangetout, topped and tailed
- 6 halves sun-dried tomatoes, shredded

Preparation: 15 minutes
Cooking time: 30 minutes

❶ Cook the onion and leek in the oil until softened but not browned, then add the squash and spices, and cook for 2 to 3 minutes more. Add the garlic, celery and pepper, then cook briefly before stirring in the bulgur wheat and apricots.

❷ Add the tomatoes, stock and seasoning, then simmer for 12 to 15 minutes, stirring occasionally.

❸ Add the mangetout and sun-dried tomatoes, and cook for 4 to 5 minutes more. Serve immediately, with a tossed green salad.

Spiced Pumpkin Soufflé

Soufflés are actually very easy to make. They don't stay light and fluffy for very long, so make sure you round up your guests on time!

SERVES 3

- 25 g/1 oz butter
- 1 Tbsp fine wholemeal flour
- 1 tsp ground cumin
- 1 tsp ground ginger
- 150 ml/¼ pint milk
- 225 g/8 oz thick pumpkin purée
- 1 tsp Dijon mustard
- 3 large eggs, separated
- Salt and ground black pepper

Preparation: 15 minutes
Cooking time: 40 minutes

❶ Preheat a 180°C/350°F/gas mark 4 oven. Lightly butter a 15–18-cm/ 6–7-inch soufflé dish.

❷ Heat the butter in a small pan, then stir in the flour with the spices and cook for 1 minute, stirring all the time. Off the heat, gradually beat in the milk, then bring slowly to the boil, stirring all the time. Cook for 1 minute, then stir in the pumpkin purée, mustard and egg yolks.

❸ Whisk the egg whites until stiff then fold them into the pumpkin mixture. Scrape the soufflé into the prepared dish. Bake for 30 to 40 minutes, until set, then serve.

Pumpkin Pancake Galette

Pumpkin, Rum and Raisin Ice Cream

Green Fruit Salad

Melon Sorbet

Date and Pumpkin Cake

Pumpkin and Prune Tart

Pumpkin and Fig Bread

Melon and Orange Compote with Almond Cake

Kabocha Bread

Squash and Apple Almond Strudel

Courgette Passion Cake

Pumpkin and Lemon Roulade

Pumpkin and Pecan Cornmeal Muffins

Pumpkin and Raisin Pie

Squash and Celery Cheese Bread

Pumpkin Pancake Galette

These flavourful pancakes are a little starchy, so they are easiest to cook in a nonstick pan.

SERVES 4

- 225 g/8 oz cooked firm-fleshed pumpkin
- 90 g/3½ oz plain flour
- 2 large eggs
- 300 ml/½ pint milk
- 1 Tbsp vegetable oil
- Pinch of salt
- Freshly grated ½ nutmeg
- Vegetable oil, for frying

TO SERVE

- Stewed apple made from 500 g/ 1 lb 2 oz cooking apples and sugar to taste
- Maple syrup

Preparation: 10 minutes

Cooking time: 15 minutes

❶ Peel and chop the cooked pumpkin, then place it in a blender or food processor with all the other batter ingredients, and blend until smooth and thick.

❷ Heat a little oil in a nonstick omelette pan, then add about one quarter of the batter. Cook the pancake until set and browned on the underside, then flip it over and cook briefly on the second side until browned. Continue until all the batter has been used.

❸ On a serving platter, layer the pancakes with the stewed apple and a generous drizzle of maple syrup. Reheat either in a microwave or a medium oven, then top with extra maple syrup before serving.

TIP

This pancake mixture also makes very good griddle cakes.

Pumpkin, Rum and Raisin Ice Cream

If you don't like rum and raisin ice cream, don't be put off, this is delicious! It is also a very good way of using up half a can of pumpkin purée!

SERVES 6–8

- 4 large egg yolks
- 1 tsp freshly grated nutmeg
- 90 g/3½ oz light muscovado sugar
- 300 ml/½ pint full-fat milk
- About 50 ml/2 fl oz dark rum
- 200 g/7 oz canned pumpkin purée
- 300 ml/½ pint single cream
- 75 g/3 oz seedless raisins

Preparation: 2½ hours
Freezing time: 4–5 hours

---

❶ Whisk together the egg yolks, nutmeg and sugar until thick. Heat the milk until almost boiling, then pour it on to the egg mixture, whisking all the time. Rinse the pan, then return the custard and cook gently until thickened just enough to coat the back of a wooden spoon. Pour the custard into a clean bowl and leave to cool completely. When cooled, chill for 1 hour.

❷ Stir the rum and pumpkin purée into the custard, then add the cream. Freeze the ice cream in a plastic box in the freezer for 4 to 5 hours, whisking or beating two or three times during freezing. Add the raisins just before the ice cream is ready. Harden the ice cream in a

suitable covered plastic container for at least 30 minutes before serving—this is necessary because of the amount of rum in the mixture.

Alternatively, you can turn into an ice-cream machine and freeze-churn until thick.

Green Fruit Salad

Refreshing and ultra-simple, all this dessert requires is a little time to prepare the fruits with care. The grapes are better skinned, if you have the inclination.

SERVES 6

- 1 small ripe Galia melon, scooped into balls
- 1 small ripe honeydew melon, scooped into balls
- 4 ripe kiwi fruits, peeled and chopped
- Green grapes – as many as you like—seeded and halved
- 1–2 Tbsp chopped fresh mint
- 2–3 Tbsp melon liqueur (optional)
- Caster sugar (optional)

Preparation: 40 minutes

Chilling time: 30 minutes

---

❶ Combine all the fruits in a large decorative serving bowl, adding any juices from the melons.

❷ Stir in the mint and the liqueur, if using. Add just a little sugar if the melons are underripe.

❸ Chill the fruits for no more than 30 minutes before serving.

TIP

If you can, use apple mint or pineapple mint in this salad. Their fruity flavours are ideal.

Melon Sorbet

I have used a Galia melon to make this light, refreshing ice but it is just as successful made with watermelon.

SERVES 6

- 350 ml/12 fl oz full-fat milk
- 75 g/3 oz caster sugar
- 300 g/11 oz Galia melon purée
- 1 Tbsp lemon juice
- 1 Tbsp chopped fresh mint

Preparation: 1 hour

Freezing time: 4–5 hours

---

❶ Heat the milk and sugar together gently until the sugar has dissolved, then bring to the boil. Simmer the syrup for 15 minutes, then pour it into a clean bowl and leave to cool completely.

❷ Blend the melon purée with the sweetened milk, lemon juice and mint. Turn the mixture into a suitable plastic containers and place in the freezer for 4 to 5 hours. Remember to stir the sorbet thoroughly twice during this time. Alternatively, turn the mixture into an ice-cream machine and freeze-churn until thick and quite firm. Serve immediately or freeze until required.

TIP

Make certain that the melon is really ripe to get the best possible flavour—it should be very fragrant through the skin, but not soft in the flesh.

---

desserts and baking

Green Fruit Salad

Date and Pumpkin Cake

Adding pumpkin purée to a cake keeps it moist and succulent. This cake is just as good as a dessert, with morning coffee or afternoon tea. I sometimes serve it with a spoonful of crème fraîche.

SERVES 8

- 90 g/3½ oz plain flour, sifted
- 1 tsp baking powder
- 1 tsp bicarbonate of soda
- 2 tsp pumpkin pie spice or mixed spice
- 75 g/3 oz dates, chopped
- 50 g/2 oz pecans, chopped
- 2 Tbsp flour
- 50 g/2 oz butter
- 175 g/6 oz light soft brown sugar
- 200 g/7 oz pumpkin purée, fresh or canned
- 2 large eggs, beaten
- Whipped cream and grated chocolate, to decorate

Preparation: 15 minutes
Cooking time: 30 minutes

❶ Preheat a 180°C/350°F/gas mark 4 oven. Line a 23-cm/9-inch round cake tin with baking parchment.

❷ Sift together the flour, raising agents and pumpkin pie spice. Mix the dates with the pecans and toss them in the 2 tablespoons flour.

❸ Melt the butter over low heat, add the sugar and stir into a thick paste. Stir in the pumpkin, then gradually add the beaten eggs. Add the dry ingredients, then beat in the floured dates and nuts. Mix thoroughly to a thick mixture, then scoop into the prepared tin.

❹ Bake in the oven for about 30 minutes, or until a skewer inserted into the centre of the cake comes out clean. Leave to cool slightly, then remove from the tin, and cool completely on a wire rack.

❺ Serve decorated with whipped cream and grated chocolate.

Pumpkin and Prune Tart

A light prune tart with a melt-in-the-mouth egg custard is one of my favourite desserts. I have now created a variation on a family recipe, and added pumpkin to the custard.

SERVES 6–8

FOR THE PASTRY

- 90 g/3½ oz butter
- 175 g/6 oz flour
- 1 tsp caster sugar
- Cold water, to mix

FOR THE FILLING

- 200 g/7 oz thick pumpkin purée, fresh or canned
- 2 large eggs, beaten
- Freshly grated ¼ nutmeg
- 3 Tbsp soft brown sugar
- 250 ml/9 fl oz milk
- 100 g/4 oz stoned, ready-to-eat prunes, chopped
- 50 g/2 oz toasted hazelnuts, chopped

Preparation: 1 hour
Cooking time: 45 minutes

❶ Prepare the pastry by blending the butter into the flour and sugar until the mixture resembles fine breadcrumbs, then add sufficient cold water to bind to a stiff dough. Knead gently on a lightly floured surface, then roll out and use to line a deep, preferably loose-based 20-cm/8-inch pie tin. Chill for 30 minutes.

❷ Preheat a 200°C/400°F/gas mark 6 oven. Spread half the pumpkin purée over the base of the pastry case, then beat the remainder with the eggs, nutmeg and brown sugar. Gradually beat in the milk. Scatter the chopped prunes and nuts over the pastry, then pour the pumpkin custard into the pastry case.

❸ Grate a little more nutmeg over the filling, then bake for 15 minutes. Lower the temperature to 190°C/ 375°F/gas mark 5 and bake for 25 to 30 minutes more, until the pastry is browned and the filling has set.

❹ Allow the tart to cool slightly, then carefully remove it from the tin. Serve warm or cold.

Pumpkin and Fig Bread

A moist fruit loaf to serve just buttered, or with jam. The figs contribute a definite flavour to the loaf, so I tend to serve it on its own, with a reviving cup of tea. I have used easy-blend dried yeast for this loaf, so it only requires one rising period.

MAKES 1 LARGE LOAF

- 500 g/1 lb 2 oz strong white bread flour
- 2 Tbsp caster sugar
- 1 tsp salt
- 1 sachet easy-blend dried yeast
- 150 g/5 oz ready-to-eat dried figs, chopped
- 225 g/8 oz thick pumpkin purée, fresh or canned
- 250 ml/9 fl oz warm water, plus extra
- Beaten egg, to glaze (optional)

Preparation: 1½ hours
Cooking time: 40 minutes

---

❶ Mix the flour, sugar and salt together in a large bowl, then stir in the dried yeast and chopped figs. Make a well in the centre, add the pumpkin purée and most of the water. Mix to a soft, manageable dough, adding extra water as necessary. Turn out onto a lightly floured surface and knead thoroughly, until the dough is smooth and elastic, 5 to 10 minutes.

❷ Shape the dough and place either on a baking sheet or in a large loaf tin. I like to make this bread in a tin—I always think the regular shape is so much easier to slice. Leave to rise for about 1 hour, covered with a damp tea towel or cling film.

❸ Preheat a 220°C/425°F/gas mark 7 oven toward the end of the rising period. Brush the loaf with a little beaten egg, if you wish—this will give a really high glaze—or sprinkle it with a little flour. Bake for 35 to 40 minutes, until the bread is well browned and the base sounds hollow when tapped. Leave to cool on a wire rack before slicing.

Melon and Orange Compote with Almond Cake

This delightful dessert is redolent of the flavours of Spain—ripe, juicy melons and oranges, almonds and fragrant, melon-scented olive oil.

SERVES 6–8

FOR THE ORANGE AND ALMOND CAKE

- 3 large eggs, separated
- 115 g/4½ oz caster sugar
- Grated rind and juice of 1 large orange
- 50 g/2 oz blanched almonds, toasted and finely chopped
- 100 g/4 oz ground almonds
- 75 g/3 oz demerara sugar
- Almond essence
- Flaked almonds, to decorate

- 1 ripe Galia melon, scooped into balls
- Pared rind of 2 large oranges
- 2–3 Tbsp extra virgin Spanish olive oil

Preparation: 40 minutes
Cooking time: 40 minutes

❶ Preheat a 180°C/350°F/gas mark 4 oven. Line a loose-based, deep, 20-cm/8-inch cake tin with baking parchment.

❷ For the cake, whisk the egg yolks with the sugar and orange rind until thick, then whisk in the chopped and ground almonds. In a separate bowl, whisk the egg whites until stiff, then fold them quickly and lightly into the mixture. Scrape and pour the cake into the cake tin, lightly level the top, then bake for about 40 minutes.

❸ Line a wire rack with baking parchment, then turn the cake out onto the rack. Take care—the cake is delicate. Let cool.

❹ Squeeze the juice from the orange and make up to 300 ml/½ pint with fresh orange juice. Heat with the demerara sugar and bring slowly to the boil, stirring to dissolve the sugar, then boil for 3 to 4 minutes until slightly syrupy. Then add a few drops of almond essence.

❺ Invert the cake onto a serving plate and prick it all over with a fine skewer. Spoon the syrup through the cake, allowing it to soak in well, then leave for at least 1 hour. Scatter with the flaked almonds.

❻ For the compote, combine the melon balls and pared orange rinds, then add the olive oil. Spoon the fruit around the almond cake. Serve cut into wedges with plenty of fruit.

desserts and baking

Kabocha Bread

Kabochas are a very popular New Zealand squash but this bread could also be made with buttercup squash.

MAKES 2 LARGE LOAVES

- 1 kabocha squash (weighing about 1 kg/2¼ lb)
- Salt and ground black pepper
- Olive oil, for drizzling
- 25 g/1 oz fresh yeast
- 300 ml/½ pint lukewarm water
- 675 g/1½ lb strong white bread flour
- 1 Tbsp salt
- 1 Tbsp Dijon mustard
- 3 Tbsp olive oil

Preparation: 2 hours
Cooking time: 40 minutes

❶ Preheat a 220°C/425°F/gas mark 7 oven. Cut the squash into six and remove the seeds, then place in a small roasting tin, and season lightly. Drizzle with olive oil and roast for 45 minutes. Leave to cool. Scoop out the flesh, then blend in a blender or food processor.

❷ Crumble the yeast into the warm water, leave for 2 to 3 minutes, then stir to make sure it has dissolved completely. Mix the flour with the salt in a large bowl and mix the mustard with the puréed squash. Make a well in the middle of the flour and add the olive oil, kabocha purée and the yeast liquid. Mix to a smooth manageable dough, adding more flour or water as necessary.

❸ Knead the dough until smooth and elastic, then flour the bowl and return the dough. Cover and leave in a warm place for about 1 hour.

❹ Turn out onto a lightly floured work surface and knead. Divide in two, then shape each piece into a long fat sausage. Place on a lightly greased and floured baking sheet, cover with a damp cloth. Leave to rise again for 30 to 40 minutes.

❺ Preheat a 220°C/425°F/gas mark 7 oven. Slash the loaves diagonally a number of times, then bake for 35 to 40 minutes, until dark golden. The base will sound hollow when tapped if they are completely cooked. Let cool on a wire rack for at least 15 minutes.

TIP

If you wish, use easy-blend dried yeast. Simply add one sachet to the flour, then shape the dough and allow one rising only.

desserts and baking

Squash and Apple Almond Strudel

I am constantly amazed at how much flavour squash will give to a dessert. An apple strudel becomes something quite different with the addition of squash—a filling but not too sweet dessert to serve after a light main course.

SERVES 6

- 25 g/1 oz butter
- 275 g/10 oz prepared kabocha squash, diced
- 1 tsp ground ginger
- Crushed seeds from 5 green cardamom pods
- 2 Tbsp soft brown sugar
- 200 g/7 oz cream cheese
- 1 sharp green eating apple, cored and cut into 5-mm/¼-in dice
- Grated rind and juice of 1 lemon
- 40 g/1½ oz toasted almonds, chopped
- 8–10 sheets filo pastry
- 50 g/2 oz butter, melted
- Sifted icing sugar, for dredging

Preparation: 20 minutes
Cooking time: 25 minutes

❶ Preheat a 200°C/400°F/gas mark 6 oven. Melt the butter in a small pan, add the squash, ginger and cardamom seeds. Cook gently for 4 to 5 minutes, until the squash is just soft, stirring occasionally. Then add the sugar.

❷ Beat the cream cheese until soft, then add the squash with the apple, lemon rind and juice, and the almonds. Mix well, then set aside.

❸ Lightly butter a baking sheet, then arrange the filo pastry sheets on it, overlapping them and stacking into a rectangle about 30 x 35 cm/ 12 x 14 inches, approximately four pastry sheets thick. Brush each pastry sheet with melted butter to keep it moist. Pile the filling in a long line in the middle of the pastry, then fold over the two sides and the bottom of the sheet. Roll the strudel up as for a spring roll, tucking the join under the strudel on the baking sheet.

❹ Brush with any remaining melted butter, then bake for 25 minutes, until the pastry is a rich golden brown. Leave to cool slightly, then transfer to a serving plate, and dredge lightly with icing sugar. Serve warm direct from the oven, or wait until cooled.

Courgette Passion Cake

Passion cake is usually made with carrots and often looks very healthy and wholesome! Despite this, it is wickedly delicious. However, for a more festive-looking cake, I add grated courgette for extra colour—use some green and some yellow if possible.

SERVES 10–12

- 250 g/9 oz plain flour
- 2 tsp baking powder
- 1 tsp bicarbonate of soda
- 1 tsp salt
- 225 g/8 oz caster sugar
- 50 g/2 oz pine nuts
- 50 g/2 oz golden raisins
- 2 ripe bananas, mashed
- 3 large eggs, beaten
- 175 g/6 oz mixed carrots and courgettes, grated
- 150 ml/¼ pint groundnut or vegetable oil

FOR THE FROSTING

- 150 g/5 oz cream cheese
- 100 g/4 oz butter, softened
- ½ tsp vanilla essence
- 225 g/8 oz icing sugar, sifted
- Grated mixed carrot and courgette, to decorate (optional)

**Preparation: 15 minutes +
45 minutes for frosting
Cooking time: 1 hour**

---

❶ Preheat a 180°C/350°F/gas mark 4 oven. Line a deep 23-cm/9-inch cake tin with baking parchment—springform is best.

❷ Sift the flour, baking powder, bicarbonate of soda and salt into a large mixing bowl, then add the sugar, pine nuts and golden raisins. Mix well, then add the mashed bananas and beaten eggs. Stir in the grated vegetables and finally the oil, then beat the cake thoroughly for 1 minute, to a thick, slightly lumpy mixture.

❸ Scrape the mixture into the prepared tin, then bake for 1 hour, or until a skewer inserted into the centre of the cake comes out clean. Leave for a few minutes, then carefully remove the cake from the tin and leave to cool completely.

❹ To make the frosting, beat the cream cheese and butter together with the vanilla until smooth, then gradually beat in the sugar. Stand in a cool place for about 30 minutes to harden slightly, then spread over the cake. A little grated mixed carrot and courgette makes a perfect decoration.

Pumpkin and Lemon Roulade

Surprisingly light and tangy, this roulade makes a very pleasant change from the more traditional pumpkin pie. An excellent dessert for the early days of autumn when a little culinary comfort is required, but nothing too heavy. I find that the best way of folding the flour into the whisked egg mixture quickly and lightly ·is with a wire whisk, not a metal spoon.

SERVES 8

- 3 large eggs
- 65 g/2½ oz caster sugar
- 65 g/2½ oz plain flour, sifted twice
- Grated rind and juice of 1 large lemon
- 150 ml/¼ pint whipping cream
- 3 Tbsp icing sugar, sifted
- 200 g/7 oz thick pumpkin purée, fresh or canned
- 50 g/2 oz seedless raisins
- Sugar, for dredging

Preparation: 15 minutes
Cooking time: 10 minutes
---

❶ Preheat a 220°C/425°F/gas mark 7 oven. Line a 33 x 23-cm/13 x 9-inch Swiss roll tin with baking parchment.

❷ Whisk the eggs and sugar together until pale and very thick—you should be able to leave a figure-of-eight from the beaters trail clearly visible in the mixture. Fold the flour and lemon rind quickly into the mixture, then scrape it into the tin, and gently level the surface, shaking it into the corners.

❸ Bake for 8 to 10 minutes, until spongy in texture and golden brown. Turn the cake onto a wire rack covered with baking parchment and sprinkled with caster sugar. Trim away the crusts of the sponge and make a shallow cut a little way in

from one of the short sides, then place another piece of parchment over the sponge. Roll it up and leave, rolled up with the paper, until cold.

❹ Whip the cream until almost stiff, then add the sugar and pumpkin. Beat well, then fold in the raisins. Unwrap the roulade and remove the inner paper. Spread the cream over the sponge, then reroll it using the sugared paper to help. Transfer to a plate.

❺ Pierce the cake right through in lots of places with a thin skewer. Drizzle the lemon juice over the roulade. Dredge with more caster sugar, then leave for about 20 minutes before serving, to allow the lemon to flavour the sponge.

Pumpkin and Pecan Cornmeal Muffins

The reason that I often add cornmeal to a muffin mix is that it makes them a little more grainy and interesting in texture. Fine polenta also works well.

MAKES 12
- 15 g/½ oz butter
- 150 g/5 oz fine wholemeal flour
- 75 g/3 oz cornmeal or fine polenta
- 1 tsp ground ginger
- 1 tsp baking powder
- ½ tsp bicarbonate of soda
- 50 g/2 oz pecans, chopped
- 1 large egg, beaten
- 175 g/6 oz thick pumpkin purée, fresh or canned
- 175 ml/6 fl oz buttermilk
- Brown sugar crystals, to decorate

Preparation: 20 minutes
Cooking time: 30 minutes

❶ Preheat a 180°C/350°F/gas mark 4 oven. Carefully line 12 deep muffin tins with muffin paper cases.

❷ Melt the butter in a small saucepan, then allow to cool. Mix together all the dry ingredients in a bowl, then add the nuts. Beat the egg with the pumpkin purée and the buttermilk, then add the melted butter. Tip the paste into the flour mixture, then mix the muffin batter together quickly, using either a metal spoon or a palette knife.

❸ Divide the mixture between the paper cases and bake for 25 to 30 minutes, until set and browned. The muffins are cooked when a fine skewer that has been inserted into them comes out clean.

❹ Scatter a few sugar crystals over each hot cake, pressing them lightly into the crumb, then leave to cool slightly before eating warm.

desserts and baking

Pumpkin and Raisin Pie

I have always loved this recipe because the pumpkin stays in slices, mixed with buttery, nutmeg-coated raisins. It makes a very unusual pie, a welcome change from traditional, custard-based recipes.

SERVES 6–8

- 675 g/1½ lb prepared pumpkin
- 100 g/4 oz demerara sugar
- Knob of butter
- 100 g/4 oz raisins
- Freshly grated nutmeg, to taste

FOR THE PASTRY

- 175 g/6 oz butter
- 350 g/12 oz fine wholemeal flour
- Pinch of salt
- Warm water, to mix

Preparation: 40 minutes
Cooking time: 40 minutes

❶ Preheat a 200°C/400°F/gas mark 6 oven. Lightly butter a deep 25-cm/10-inch pie plate.

❷ Cut the pumpkin into 2.5-cm/1-inch pieces, then slice them thinly. Layer the pumpkin with the sugar in a saucepan and dot with slivers of butter. Cover the pan, then cook over low heat for 10 to 12 minutes. Shake the pan occasionally to stop the pumpkin from burning.

❸ Blend the butter into the flour and salt until the mixture resembles fine breadcrumbs, then mix to a firm but manageable dough with warm water. Knead on a floured surface, then divide into two. Roll out one half to line the pie plate.

❹ Stir the raisins into the pumpkin with a generous amount of freshly grated nutmeg. Pile the filling into the pastry case, scooping it from the pan with a slotted spoon. Reserve the juices to serve with the pie. Roll out the remaining pastry and use to cover the pie, damping the edges to seal together. Crimp the edges.

❺ Bake for 35 to 40 minutes, until well browned. Serve cut into slices with custard or cream, and the pumpkin juices spooned over.

TIP

This pie is made with a wholemeal pastry. It is much easier to bind a wholemeal dough with warm water, rather than cold.

Squash and Celery Cheese Bread

A squash picnic loaf that is really a meal in itself, but is also delicious with a soft creamy cheese—a goat's cheese would be my first choice. I love the combination of the celery and squash—it works really well.

MAKES 1 LOAF

- 4 sticks celery
- 1 garlic clove, quartered
- 150 ml/¼ pint water
- 275 g/10 oz wholemeal bread flour
- 250 g/9 oz strong white flour
- ½ tsp salt
- 15 g/½ oz fresh yeast
- 175 g/6 oz cold roast squash (use a firm-fleshed variety, such as crown prince or acorn), diced
- 75 g/3 oz Cheddar cheese, grated

Preparation: 2½ hours
Cooking time: 40 minutes

---

❶ Reserve any leaves from the celery, then chop the sticks finely. Place in a small pan with the garlic and water, and bring to the boil. Cover the pan and simmer for 10 minutes. Drain and reserve the water, making it up to 350 ml/ 12 fl oz with cold water. Set the celery aside.

❷ Sift the flours together with the salt into a bowl. Crumble the yeast into the luke warm celery-flavoured water, leave for 2 to 3 minutes, then stir to make sure the yeast has dissolved. Add the liquid to the flours, then mix to a manageable dough. Knead thoroughly for about 10 minutes, until the dough is smooth, then return to the bowl, and cover with a damp cloth or cling film. Leave in a warm place for about 1 hour, until doubled in size.

❸ Meanwhile, mix the squash and celery with the grated cheese and season generously.

❹ Scrape the dough out of the bowl, knead lightly, then divide into two. Roll out each piece into a 23-cm/9-inch circle, then place one round on a lightly greased or floured baking sheet. Pile the squash filling onto the bread, then damp the rim of the dough and cover with the remaining bread. Pinch the edges of the dough together to seal, then cover and leave in a warm place for 30 to 40 minutes, until risen.

❺ Preheat a 220°C/425°F/gas mark 7 oven. Scatter a little white flour over the loaf, then bake for 40 minutes. Leave to cool for at least 15 minutes on a wire rack before cutting into rough wedges to serve.

Index

Acorn Soup, Roasted, with Cucumber
Salsa 19
Acorn Squash with Lentil & Celery
Sauce 94

Banana Squash, Curried 100
Beef, Rich Daube of, with Baby Patty Pan
Squash 78
Beef, Squash & Mustard Pie 76
Beef & Squash Stew, Spiced, with Cous
Cous 77
Blue Cheese & Pecan Risotto with
Squash 104
Bulgur Wheat, Squash, & Cucumber
Salad 48
Butternut & Chicken Liver Pâté 32
Butternut & Orange Soup 20
Butternut Squash, Roasted Lamb with 75
Butternut Squash & Cauliflower Bake 96

Chicken, Mexican, Baked Onion Squash
with 86
Chicken, Pumpkin Pizza with 88
Chicken Liver Pâté, Butternut & 32
Chicken & Courgette Sauce for Pasta 90
Chicory, Tomato, & Melon Salad 44
Chilli Bean & Pumpkin Salad 49
Cod, Spicy Pumpkin Stuffed 59
Courgette
    Baked Limed Courgettes in Cream 26
    Chicken & Courgette Sauce for Pasta
    90
    Mixed Fish Cakes with Courgette
    Salad 64
    Pumpkin Plaice with Courgette
    Sauce 63
    Shrimp & Courgette Lasagne 54
    Spiced Courgette & Roast Squash
    Salad 47
    Spinach & Courgette Pie 95
    Squash & Courgette Trout 67
    Courgette & Fresh Tuna Risotto 58
    Courgette Passion Cake 121

Courgette & Squash Ratatouille with
Melon 50
Crab, Almond & Pumpkin Curry 56
Crown Prince Squash, Roast, & Pistachio
Pâté 28
cucumbers 9,10
    Apple & Cucumber Salsa 68
    Chilled Cucumber & Green Chilli
    Soup 18
    Cucumber & Radish Raita 34
    Cucumber Salad with Spiced Pork &
    Sesame Seeds 40
    Cucumber Salsa 19
    Pasta Salad Verde 41
    Squash, Cucumber & Bulgur Wheat
    Salad 48

Date & Pumpkin Cake 114
Duck, Confit of, with Gingered Pumpkin
83–5

Fish Cakes, Mixed, with Courgette
Salad 64
Fisherman's Pumpkin Pie 65

Gem Squash, Baked, with Parmesan
Cream 24
Gem Squash Salad 44
Green Fruit Salad 112

Haddock with Spaghetti Squash, Hot
Chilli 62
Ham Rolls, Kabocha & Celery Stuffed 80

Kabocha, Fennel & Orange Casserole 107
Kabocha Bread 118
Kabocha & Celery Stuffed Ham Rolls 80

Lamb, Roast, with Butternut Squash 75
Lamb, Spiced, with Pumpkin &
Chick Peas 74
Lamb & Pumpkin Koftas, Curried 29
Lamb & Pumpkin Moussaka 72

Mackerel, Grilled, with Apple &
Cucumber Salsa 68
Mediterranean Baked Stuffed Squash 97
Mediterranean Roasted Pumpkin Soup 20
melons 9,10
    Belgian Endive, Tomato, & Melon
    Salad 44
    Courgette & Squash Ratatouille with
    Melon 50
    Green Fruit Salad 112
    Melon, Grape & Chicken Salad 39
    Melon with Figs & Parma Ham 26
    Melon & Orange Compote with
    Almond Cake 117
    Melon & Pesto Soup 22
    Melon Sorbet 112
    Spiced Minted Melon Balls 30
Mexican Chilli with Spicy Squash 73
Monkfish & Pumpkin, Roast, with
Rice 57
Mushroom & Patty Pan Salad, Warm 42
Mussels & Squash with Tomato
Spaghetti 66

Onion Squash, Baked, with Mexican
Chicken 86

Passion Cake, Courgette 121
Pasta Salad Verde 41
Patty Pan Squash, Baby, Rich Daube of
Beef with 78
Patty Pan Squash, Baked Stuffed 102
Patty Pan & Warm Mushroom Salad 42
Patty Pans, Baby, Scallops & Bacon
with 69
Pepper & Squash, Roasted, Salad 46
Plaice, Pumpkin, with Courgette Sauce 63
Pork, Pot-Roasted, with Squash 82
Pork Fillet, Normandy, with Apples &
Squash 81
Prawn, Squash with 55
Prawn & Courgette Lasagne 54
pumpkins 8, 9, 11, 14, 15

Index / Acknowledgements

Chilli Bean & Pumpkin Salad 49

Confit of Duck with Gingered Pumpkin
  83–5

Crab, Almond & Pumpkin Curry 56

Date & Pumpkin Cake 114

Fisherman's Pumpkin Pie 65

Lamb & Pumpkin Moussaka 72

Mediterranean Roast Pumpkin Soup 20

Pumpkin, Bacon & Tomato Skewers 27

Pumpkin, Carrot & Lovage Soup 24

Pumpkin, Lentil & Bacon Soup 22

Pumpkin, Rum & Raisin Ice
  Cream 111

Pumpkin Chutney 30

Pumpkin & Fig Bread 116

Pumpkin & Lemon Roulade 122

Pumpkin & Haricot Bean
  Cassoulet 101

Pumpkin Pancake Galette 110

Pumpkin & Pecan Cornmeal
  Muffins 124

Pumpkin Pizza with Chicken 88

Pumpkin Plaice with Courgette Sauce
  63

Pumpkin & Prune Tart 115

Pumpkin & Raisin Pie 125

Pumpkin Relish 34

pumpkin seeds, toasting 15

Pumpkin & Spinach Salad with Feta
  Cheese 52

Roast Pumpkin, Tomato & Aubergine
  Salad 36

Roast Pumpkin Ratatouille Cobbler
  98–9

Savoury Country Pumpkin Pie 106

Spiced Lamb with Pumpkin &
  Chickpeas 74

Spiced Pumpkin Soufflé 108

Spicy Pumpkin Stuffed Cod 59

Squid & Pumpkin Stew with
  Tomatoes 70

Turkey, Pumpkin & Cranberry Pie 91

Warm Roasted Pumpkin & Green Bean
  Salad 41

Sardines, Grilled, with Spaghetti
  Squash 60

Sausage, Roast, & Squash, with Red
  Cabbage 79

Scallops with Baby Patty Pans & Bacon 69

Spaghetti Squash, Broiled Sardines
  with 60

Spaghetti Squash, Hot Chili Haddock
  with 62

Spinach & Courgette Pie 95

squash 8, 9, 12–15

  Beef, Squash & Mustard Pie 76

  Blue Cheese & Pecan Risotto with
    Squash 104

  Mediterranean Baked Stuffed Squash 97

  Mexican Chili with Spicy Squash 73

  Mussels & Squash with Tomato
    Spaghetti 66

  Normandy Pork Fillet with Apples &
    Squash 81

  Pot-Roasted Pork with Squash 82

  Roast Squash, Vegetable & Pasta
    Salad 38

  Roasted Bell Pepper & Squash Salad 46

  Roasted Sausage & Squash with Red
    Cabbage 79

  Spiced Beef & Squash Stew with
    Couscous 77

  Spiced Courgette & Roasted Squash
    Salad 47

  Squash & Almond Apple Strudel 120

  Squash & Apricot Bulgur Risotto 108

  Squash & Celery Cheese Bread 126

  Squash & Okra Curry 105

  Squash with Prawns 55

  Squash Stuffed Roasted Pepper 100

  Squash & Courgette Ratatouille with
    Melon 50

  Squash & Courgette Trout 67

  Turkey & Squash Fricassée 92

  see also under Acorn; Banana; Butternut;
    Crown Prince; Gem; Kabocha;
    Onion; Patty Pan & Spaghetti Squash

Squid & Pumpkin Stew with Tomatoes 70

Trout, Squash & Courgette 67

Tuna Risotto, Fresh, Courgette & 58

Turkey, Pumpkin & Cranberry Pie 91

Turkey & Squash Fricassée 92

Acknowledgements

This book is dedicated to Mr and Mrs
Upton of Slindon, West Sussex, Pioneering
Pumpkin Growers Extraordinaire, who
have been so generous to me with their
time, their knowledge, and above all, their
enthusiasm. The publishers would like to
thank Philip Wilkins and Jon Bouchier for
photography.

Picture Credits

p.6, Life File, pp.7, 8, 11, 12, 13, 49, 66,
74, 76, 120, 128, Japics Photographic.